Charles Dickens

WEST LOTHIAN COUNTY COUNCIL

Education Committee

Linlithgow Academy School

SESSION 19.69 197.0.

AWARDED TO

DAVID WATSON

Class VI

General Excellence Prize

donated by Mr. Easton

J. C. Huston

Headmaster.

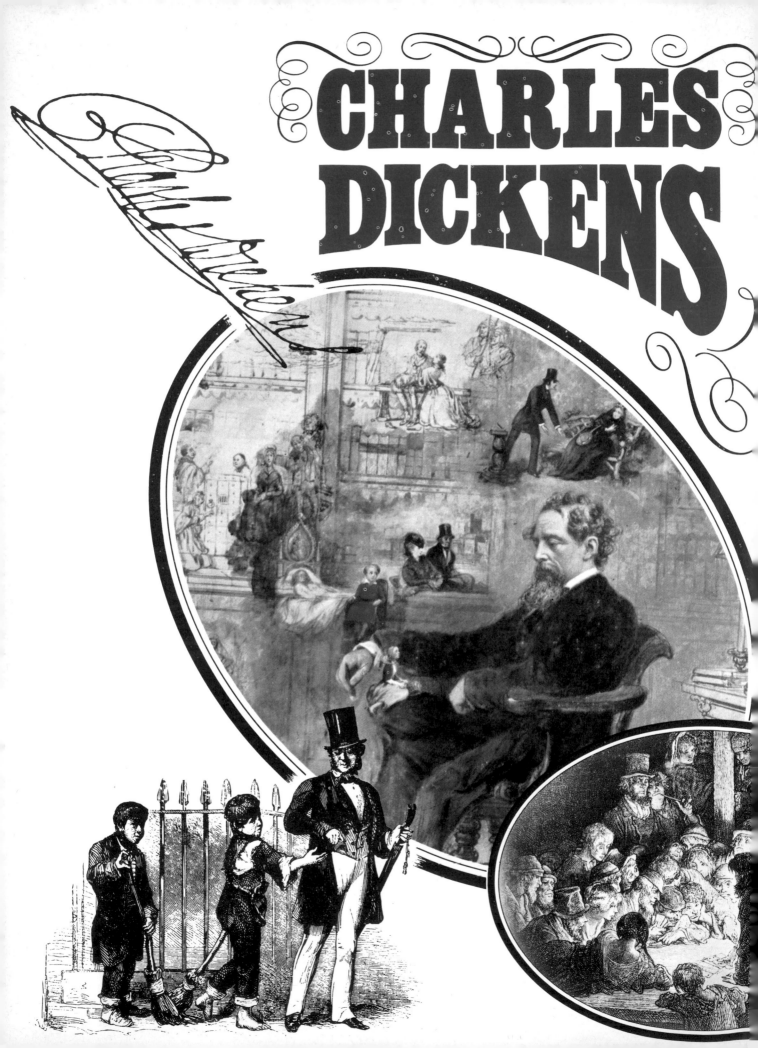

CHARLES DICKENS

AN AUTHENTIC ACCOUNT OF HIS LIFE & TIMES BY MARTIN FIDO

HAMLYN

Published by The Hamlyn Publishing Group Ltd.
London, New York, Sydney and Toronto
Hamlyn House, The Centre,
Feltham, Middlesex.
SBN 600 031 853
All rights reserved
Phototype set by Filmtype Services,
Scarborough, Yorkshire
Printed in Italy by O.G.A.M. Verona

Contents

Introduction

1812-1870, the lifespan of Charles Dickens, was a period of astonishing change. In 1812 Napoleon was thrust back from Russia and the French domination of Europe began to crumble. In 1870 Bismarck overthrew Napoleon's brittle nephew, and the scene was set for the twentieth century with Germany as the leading commercial and military power on the continent. In 1812 'Farmer George' was on the throne and the Prince Regent was setting a tone of eighteenth-century elegance and gusto in London society; in 1870 Queen Victoria had reigned for thirty years and was to consolidate the heavy respectability of the Victorians over the next thirty. When Dickens was born the parson and the squire dominated the lives of many of his fellow countrymen, and the hereditary aristocracy with their huge estates ruled the country through a parliament which they controlled. In 1870 the franchise had been extended to working men, Disraeli and Gladstone led parties which depended on their appeal to a democratic electorate for power, and the great industrialists exerted more influence on policy than the landowners. Steamships, railway trains and wireless telegraphy replaced sailing ships, stagecoaches and horse-delivered mail in the course of Dickens' lifetime. Towns which had played no significant part in

Left above:
Two prints of ferocious eighteenth-century revolutionaries, the kind respectable Englishmen remembered with uneasiness, lest their example incite violence among the poor.

Left:
By the mid-century, the only form of public transport using the horse were carts and omnibuses, like the one shown here in Life in a London Omnibus, *by W. M. Egley, 1859.*

earlier English history grew into the vital cities on which the wealth of England depended as coal, steel and power milling brought importance to Manchester, Sheffield, Leeds and Liverpool.

Change for the nation meant change for individuals. Huge fortunes were amassed by business men until the wealthiest of them outshone all but the very greatest of the old estate-owning families. The poor, who had hitherto controlled their own lives in independent cottage industries, now moved to the big cities and found employment in the growing factories. Where work was not to be found, city slums, choked and blackened with soot from factory chimneys, took the place of the rural hovels and cabins of the past. Poverty was always present and could be terrible, Men, women and children dressed in filthy rags, with no shoes, obviously starving to death, were a sight any Londoner might expect to see in the poorer districts. Drink was cheap; many of the poor used it as a soporific drug to escape their misery. Crime was another way out. Daylight robbery, shoplifting and pickpocketing were commonplace events. The Haymarket was thronged with prostitutes and gaudy brothels studded the West End of London.

The Victorians could see no easy solution to these problems, but they attacked the symptoms vigorously. Sir Robert Peel's police force was laughed at when it was introduced, but soon came to be accepted. Dickens was typical of respectable men of his time in the admiration he had for the police as public servants. Much as he hated poverty, he hated disorder on the streets even more and was prepared to take the time to bring charges against pickpockets and disorderly women.

Religion was called into the lists to combat public immorality and the uncharitable toleration of other people's misery. The Evangelical movement called upon individuals to make their own lives more and more narrowly virtuous and did much to determine the stiflingly sober tone of middle-class Victorian society. It tended, however, to substitute emotional fervour for intellectual theology and encouraged an increasing use of a canting jargon, drawn from echoes of the bible, as evidence of practising Christianity. Many, Dickens among them, were offended by a religion which laid more emphasis on saving the souls of the poor than serving their bodily needs.

The Crimean War in the eighteen-fifties shattered all confidence in the old ruling-class establishment. The government's sheer incompetence in organising the transport and equipment of an army astounded the nation. An Administrative Reform Association, founded by Dickens and other writers, was short-lived, but the necessity of meeting its demands was recognised, and after the war competition and promotion by ability replaced the old systems of nepotism and jobbery in the army and civil service.

Dickens played a leading part in the public protest against squalor, vice, disease and complacency about these things in his time. He told his readers how the face of England was being changed for the worse: in *The Old Curiosity Shop* he described the road between Birmingham and Wolverhampton with its huge throbbing engine-houses, tall chimney stacks belching black smoke and flames across the countryside, and smoking slagheaps glowing dully from the live cinders pitched onto them; in *Hard Times* he painted a drab new cotton city, its river stained with industrial waste, its buildings square and joyless, and its monotonous, rattling machinery seeming to parody the life which was drained from its inhabitants. He took his readers to the back streets and showed them men corrupted by their foul surroundings, who lived by preying on the innocent. He exposed the conditions that bred disease, and warned that contagion, once let loose, was no respector of class or wealth.

'There have been at work among us three great social agencies:' said a nonconformist preacher in the eighteen-forties, 'the London City Mission; the novels of Mr. Dickens; the cholera.'

Yet the typical educated Victorian did not find that his immediate response to the life around him was guilt at the wretchedness it displayed, nor even fear of revolution as a consequence (although the French Revolution had certainly led many Englishmen to fear that a similar rising might take place at home in the first half of the nineteenth century). Dickens and his readers found many causes for self-congratulation in the life they enjoyed.

Technological advances brought faster travel, cheaper and more durable goods, and the rapid dissemination of news to those rich enough to enjoy such things. And there was greater social mobility as industrial expansion turned more traders into business gentlemen, which opened such enjoyment up to many who would previously have been disqualified

Lord George Gordon, from an eighteenth-century print.

Right:
A satire on the English class system, 1838.

on class grounds. Scientific progress was sweeping away the superstitions of the past; British naval and military strength gave the population a profound sense of security and superiority.

Here again, Dickens reflected the confidence of his times. He could write nostalgically of the stagecoaches he remembered as a boy, but he knew well enough that he preferred the comfort of trains running on time. He believed that his ability would have carried him to the top of any society into which he might have been born, but his contentment with living in nineteenth-century England rested on a profound conviction that the past was in every way inferior. He adapted easily to changing times because he wanted the changes.

Charles Dickens offered the nineteenth century, as he offers us, the rich, vivid, comic, tragic world of his imagination. But he lived as rich and vivid a life himself in a world he made as comic and found as tragic. It is a part of this world which he has reflected back for us in his writings.

THE TREE OF TAXATION.

(FROM THE NORTHERN LIBERATOR OF AUGUST 13, 1838.)

THE above Engraving will give a visible representation of the MANNER in which the Taxing System works.

The Community may be divided into FOUR classes. The pockets of the FIRST, or Highest Class, escape from the Roots of the Tax Tree altogether—they get back, in the shape of Windfalls, more than they pay. The pockets of the SECOND Class the Roots touch but lightly. The THIRD, or Labouring Class, is the source of the whole nourishment drawn up by the Tax Tree. The FOURTH Class, the very Poor, it touches but to destroy.

NEWCASTLE UPON TYNE: PRINTED AT THE NORTHERN LIBERATOR OFFICE, 49, SIDE, BY JOHN BELL.

The Boy in the Blacking Factory

On a spring day in 1824 a small boy and a man walked from the Strand to a ramshackle warehouse over-looking the river at Hungerford Stairs. Here blacking was manufactured, and here the boy was to be employed in labelling the pots in which the blacking was sold, first with oil-paper, and then with blue paper, the whole tied round neatly with string and then clipped trim. The man was James Lamert, the manager of the blacking factory. His brother-in-law, George, owned the business which rivalled the famous Warren's Blacking, 30, The Strand, a household word in the early nineteenth century. The Lamerts printed Hungerford Stairs in the address on their blacking pot label very small so that WARREN'S BLACKING, 30 Hungerford Stairs, STRAND, might be mistaken for the better known brand.

The boy was Charles Dickens, and his father's habitual extravagance was now reaching the stage at which debtors' prison loomed ahead. Lamert, who was distantly related to the boy, and lodged with his family, had brought him to find employment in the blacking factory as an act of kindness. Sending the eldest boy out to work seemed one of the few ways in which the family could lighten the domestic budget, and bring in a little more money. For a short time Charles was given lessons by James Lamert in the lunch hours, but this soon ceased, and with the removal of the factory to Chandos Street Charles felt that his humiliation was complete when he and another boy were set to work in the factory window for passers-by to watch. 'No words', he wrote later, 'can express the secret agony of my soul as I sunk into this companionship; compared these everyday associates with those of my happier childhood; and felt my early hopes of growing up to be a learned and distinguished man crushed in my breast.'

Readers of *David Copperfield* may recognise the situation, for David working in Murdstone and Grinby's warehouse parallels the boy Dickens, work-ing in the blacking factory at Hungerford Stairs. The associates deplored by the adult Dickens—in real life their names were Bob Fagin and Paul Green—reappear in *David Copperfield* as Mick Walker and Mealy Potatoes. David, like Dickens, bewails his own loss of education. 'I know enough of the world now', he says, 'to have almost lost the capacity of being much surprised by anything; but it is a matter of some surprise to me, even now, that I can have been so easily thrown away at such an age. A child of excellent abilities, and with strong powers of observa-tion, quick, eager, delicate, and soon hurt bodily or mentally, it seems wonderful to me that nobody should have made any sign on my behalf. But none was made; and I became, at ten years old, a little labouring hind.' How revealing it is that Dickens should take two years off his age in transferring his experience to David! Being sent to work at the age of twelve was indeed for Dickens a memorable and traumatic experience.

Yet worse things can happen to a child than being sent out to work. No excessive sympathy colours David Copperfield's account of his comrades at Murdstone and Grinby's, and David's own experience is rendered horrible largely by the fact that it is the Murdstones who have dismissed him to the ware-house in the hope that he may be forgotten, and self-supporting, a charge upon their purses and the world's affection no longer. Dickens himself experienced no such outright rejection. Why then did his very brief experience in the blacking factory—two or three months at the most—leave so indelible a mark on his mind?

To understand its importance to him we must

understand three things. In the first place, the blacking factory episode was the one outstanding incident in his boyhood. John Dickens, his father, was an unremarkable naval pay clerk, reasonably good at his job, hard working and conscientious, only distinguished by his total inability to live within his income. Until 1824 the child's life had been disrupted by no more than the occasional moves consequent upon his father's employment. Portsea–London–Chatham–London again : moves like these hardly proved unsettling to the small boy whose father was a stimulating companion, unfailingly affectionate, and as generous as it lay within his means to be. It was his father who brought home the cheap reprints of eighteenth-century novels : *Robinson Crusoe, Joseph Andrews, Tom Jones, Tristram Shandy, Roderick Random, Peregrine Pickle* and *Humphrey Clinker,* as well as the much loved *Arabian Nights* and *Tales of the Genji,* which gave the child endless delight. It was John Dickens too, who told the young Charles that if he worked very hard he might one day own Gad's Hill Place, the large house outside Rochester which indeed became the novelist's final home. It was only in 1824 that John Dickens' inability to balance his household budget can have begun to affect his son's life. Then, indeed, all life must truly have seemed disturbed. Creditors beating on the door and calling down the passage ; John Dickens cowering upstairs, afraid to venture out lest he should be arrested ; Elizabeth Dickens announcing on a plate at the door the establishment of her school (to which nobody came). Most distressing of all, the boy was first taken from school and then sent out to work.

With the sense of urgency created by this domestic crisis, the boy also experienced what seemed to him desertion by his family. For his humiliation did not save the family finances ; within two weeks John

Old Hungerford Stairs. To the left is the decaying warehouse which was taken over by the blacking factory where Dickens worked as a boy.

Below :
The kind of blacking pot Dickens labelled.

Dickens was arrested and taken to the Marshalsea prison, where his wife and children joined him. Charles alone was left outside the prison, earning his own living, supporting himself in digs. Now he suffered the humiliation of seeing his sister Fanny continue her useful musical education, while he himself was truly a 'little labouring hind' in a dead-end job, keeping himself on six shillings a week. Catastrophic events, Dickens learnt, left the individual fighting for himself: he was later to prove one of the most profoundly independent and economically aggressive writers in the history of English literature. Nor did the experience of rejection end with his father's prison sentence. Although a small legacy set John Dickens at large, Charles continued to contribute his six shillings a week to the family finances until his father quarrelled with the Lamerts, and Charles was removed to school. Removed though, with a sense of betrayal he was never to lose, for his mother hoped still that he might return to the factory. 'I never afterwards forgot, I shall never forget, I never can forget, that my mother was warm for my being sent back.'

The fear of losing his class standing was the last vital element in this experience for Dickens. His family position was not altogether secure: his grandparents had been in domestic service and this shameful family secret was not revealed until after his death. His maternal grandfather had suffered self-exile to escape the consequences of petty embezzlement. Just as the Dickenses finally hoped to respect themselves as a gentlemanly family, Charles had found himself threatened with relegation to the working classes. For the Victorian middle-class citizen this loss of status carried with it the threat of losing all opportunities for cultural advancement, all opportunities for economic security, and all hope of being, as Charles said, 'a learned and distinguished man'. For the rest of his life Dickens' touchy sense of his own honour was to be compounded with a prickly unease about his class status, and while he shared many of the moral views of the Victorian bourgeoisie, he was never able to share their complacent and secure sense of position.

From Clerk
to Journalist

Within three years of his release from prison John Dickens was again in financial difficulty. Charles, now aged fifteen, was therefore removed from school and once again set to work. But this time he started on a middle-class career commensurate with his education and holding out serious prospects. He went as a lawyer's clerk to the firm of Ellis and Blackmore in Gray's Inn.

It is curious to note that the first three jobs Dickens undertook in his working life all served to disillusion him with aspects of the British Establishment. At Ellis and Blackmore's he enjoyed the rowdy social life of the young clerks, visiting the theatre and getting drunk with his friend Thomas Potter, but he also developed a hearty contempt for solicitors, their offices, and all their ways, which was to stay with him for life and to leave its mark in numerous novels. Stuffy lawyers are to be found as frequently as lively clerks throughout his work. And it was not merely the unattractiveness of a middle-aged lawyer's life to an ambitious young man which repelled Dickens; Disraeli's dismissive remark—'The Bar? Pooh! Law and bad jokes until one is forty' – would only represent a part of Dickens' feelings about the legal profession. To him the distinction between legality and justice, the essence of legal business, would always seem little but a humbug.

To a young man with Dickens' ability and application the challenge of changing career before he was seventeen was easily met. Here again his father's life influenced his own. John Dickens, forcibly retired from the Navy Pay Office as a former insolvent, had set himself to work at the age of forty-one to master shorthand, and had found himself an appointment as a parliamentary journalist. Charles, scenting a more interesting future than the law promised, spent almost

a week's salary on the purchase of Gurney's *Brachygraphy, or an Easy and Compendious System of Shorthand*, and in less than a year had mastered the art sufficiently to find employment as a shorthand reporter. The application and self-discipline required for this were remarkable. To Gurney his *Brachygraphy* might seem easy; to Charles it was 'a sea of perplexity'. 'A thing like the beginning of a cobweb meant expectation', he wrote in *David Copperfield*, 'and a pen and ink skyrocket stood for disadvantageous' (The sample words are significant).

But admirable as Charles' mastery of shorthand was, it was not yet adequate for him to embark upon a journalistic career. For a short while he remained within the confines of the law as a shorthand reporter in Doctors Commons. This was an anachronistic branch of the courts, later reformed out of sight and its business taken over by the Probate Divorce and Admiralty Division of the High Court. Here the contempt for lawyers which Charles had already learnt at Ellis and Blackmore's was strengthened. In later life he observed that Doctors Commons had been about two hundred years out of date, and called it 'a little out of the way place where they administer what is called ecclesiastical law, and play all kinds of tricks with obsolete old monsters of acts of parliament, which three-fourths of the world know nothing about and the other fourth supposes to have been dug up in a fossil state in the days of the Edwards'. Dickens was always

Right, above:
City clerks at a chophouse; an illustration by Phiz for Bleak House.
Right:
The old House of Commons, with the reporter's gallery where Dickens worked as a young journalist.

Dickens shared the view of this cartoonist of the period, that politicians were bores and parliament a sleepy talking shop.

Right :
The Eatanswill election, described in Pickwick Papers, *was based on Dickens' own experience of corrupt electioneering. Illustrated by Cruickshank.*

a very modern-minded man, and the hallowed tradition under lying ancient British institutions only served to confirm his contempt for them.

On his eighteenth birthday Dickens took out a reader's ticket to the British Museum, where he completed his education to his own satisfaction. His dissatisfaction with his career led him to apply for a job in the theatre. But before he could attend an audition he was offered an opening in journalism. An uncle of his had begun a periodical containing verbatim parliamentary reports, the *Mirror of Parliament*. John Dickens was already working for the *Mirror*, and Charles immediately joined the reporting staff when given the opportunity.

Once again, a great British institution was exhibited to the young man, and left him unmoved and hostile. Parliament seemed to him an empty talking shop;

politicians were stupid, hypocritical, insensitive windbags. Nevertheless the young man's career was brilliant. He was soon established as one of the fastest and most accurate shorthand reporters squeezed into the Strangers' Gallery, and soon he was enrolled on the staff of the *Morning Chronicle, The Times'* Liberal rival. Now he was no longer confined to the gallery, but was sent across the country to report speeches in the great Reform debate wherever they might take place.

Dashing madly in chaises from remote country towns to London, transcribing his shorthand notes as he went, Dickens contributed to the instantaneous publication with which the *Chronicle* hoped to threaten *The Times'* circulation. He was well paid for reporting elections in the unreformed boroughs, and was granted a generous expense account. 'I have charged for broken hats, broken luggage, broken chaises, broken harness—everything but a broken head which is about the only thing they would have grumbled to pay for', he later recalled.

But in 1833, he took the first step towards the career which was to lead him to greatness. In such spare time as was available he had written a humorous short story called 'A Sunday out of Town' and had hopefully dropped it through the letter-box of the *Monthly Magazine*. This journal accepted unsolicited contributions, and paid its contributors nothing. It was a suitably humble outlet for the opening of a literary career. An unknown sub-editor altered Dickens's title to 'A Dinner at Poplar Walk' and the career of Charles Dickens as a writer of fiction had begun. The magazine now invited Dickens to send more material and he sent two more stories to which, for the first time, he appended the pseudonym 'Boz'. His younger brother, Augustus, had been nicknamed Moses after the character in *The Vicar of Wakefield*, and this had been facetiously shortened to the name by which Dickens was to become known to the public.

The identity of 'Boz' was no secret among journalists. The *Morning Chronicle* and the *Evening Chronicle* began to print his sketches. Harrison Ainsworth, whose sensational historical novels were at this time hugely successful, arranged a meeting with 'Boz' and introduced him to his publisher John McCrone. McCrone had the idea of collecting Boz's sketches and publishing them in a volume illustrated by the established caricaturist George Cruikshank. Dickens was delighted and agreed to write sufficient sketches to fill two volumes. He willingly agreed to sell the copyright of this first publication for £150.

The first volume of sketches was published on 7 February 1836, was well received by the reviewers, and suddenly it seemed that everyone was asking Dickens to write something. He was preparing material for a second volume of sketches ; he was still working for the *Chronicle* ; he was preparing to write the libretto for an operetta ; he had promised to write a one act farce ; and, not recognising the vital step in his career, he had undertaken to write a text to accompany a series of sporting prints by Robert Seymour, the comic artist.

The Election at Eatanswill.

DINNER DRESS.

Maria Beadnell

In 1829, while he was still a young shorthand reporter with no very clear prospects, Dickens had met and fallen in love with Maria Beadnell, the daughter of a wealthy banker. Maria was a lively, petite charmer. All the empty accomplishments of a well-to-do young lady were hers: she played the harp and she kept an album in which her admirers might sketch and write, as Dickens did, feeble verses. She enjoyed the attentions of young men, but lavished her own attention on her liver and white spaniel, which was spoiled with mutton chops from which the fat had been cut off. Dickens became so infatuated with Maria that he even managed to feel affection for Daphne, this pampered animal, which reappeared as Jip in *David Copperfield*.

Mr and Mrs Beadnell paid little attention to the young man at first. He was younger than Maria, and so little did they regard him as a serious suitor for her that Mrs Beadnell never even learnt to pronounce his name correctly, calling him throughout their acquaintance 'Mr Dickin'. Until 1831 Dickens was free to feel that his entire happiness centred on Maria, and she obviously enjoyed the presence of an admirer who bowed to her smallest whim.

But towards the end of 1831 Mr Beadnell apparently discovered that John Dickens had once been in the Marshalsea. This fact, combined with the enormous social gulf which at that time lay between bankers and journalists, led the Beadnells to send Maria to Paris in the hope that her friendship with Dickens might be casually terminated. From their point of view and Maria's the manoeuvre was an entire success. On her return, she ceased to give the young reporter the encouragement which he felt was merited by his strenuous efforts to carve out a career for himself.
Fashion plate, 1829.

In 1832 Dickens was trying to use Maria's best friend, Marianne Leigh, as a go-between. This involved uneasy manoeuvring; in March he was telling Miss Leigh that he called at the Beadnells specifically to fetch *her*. Moreover Marianne Leigh was not a girl with whom manoeuvring was safe. She enjoyed gossip and scandal, had a tantalising, reproachful and flirtatious manner with young men, and may even have been interested in winning Charles' affections for herself. By 1833 these young people had their emotional affairs in a frenzied tangle of cross purposes and recriminations. Maria seems to have cared little: on Charles' twenty-first birthday she snubbed him and called him a mere 'boy'. Marianne's feelings, as indeed her whole part in this intrigue, can only be guessed at. But at March of 1833 Dickens was coldly and stiffly returning Maria's letters to her, and two months later he terminated their acquaintance with some gauche but wounded notes attempting to sort out for Maria's benefit what his relations with Marianne had been.

The whole affair seems about as preposterous as those portrayed in the girls' illustrated romantic magazines of our own day. But Charles Dickens had the sensitivity of an artist, and even calf love could remain a life-long painful memory for him. He put Maria into his books: she is Dolly Varden and David Copperfield's wife Dora. But he could never bring himself to tell anyone of the pain she had caused him, and burnt the autobiographical fragment in which he had described it truthfully, fearing even to let posterity know how intensely he had been hurt by an extremely ordinary flirtatious girl. Twenty years later she briefly reappeared in his life, and Dickens' immediate and passionate response to hearing from her again showed how powerful she had lived in his memory.

The Birth of Pickwick

'Chapman and Hall have made me an offer of *fourteen pounds a month* to write and edit a new publication they contemplate, entirely by myself; to be published monthly and each number to contain four wood cuts. I am to make my estimate and calculation, and to give them a decisive answer on Friday morning. . . . the emolument is too tempting to resist.'

In these words Dickens told the girl who was to become his wife of the latest piece of work to fall his way. His words made clear how coldly economic was his interest in this new publication; until the publishers put forward their proposal it had never occurred to him to write any such book. Chapman and Hall had tried in vain to persuade other writers, including Theodore Hook and Henry Mayhew, to produce the accompanying text for the series of comic cockney sporting prints concerning the adventures of an imaginary Nimrod Club which they proposed to publish for Robert Seymour. Mayhew and Hook had no need of 'the emolument' which could 'tempt' Dickens. But the young man, hoping to marry soon, was willing to accept the new commitment in return for the temporary guaranteed addition to his income.

Nevertheless, the forceful personality of the young hack writer instantly imprinted itself on the established caricaturist's project. Objecting, truthfully enough, that he was 'no great sportsman, except in regard to all kinds of locomotion', and suggesting that 'it would be infinitely better for the plates to arrive naturally out of the text', Dickens had easily persuaded William Hall, the junior partner in the publishing firm, to transfer from Seymour to the writer the creative responsibility of determining the nature of the works they were to produce jointly. With this freedom to write his own book, Dickens said, 'I thought of Mr Pickwick.'

But did he? He *remembered* the name of Moses Pickwick, the celebrated Bath coach proprietor. He sketched a simple burlesque of 'parliamentary' proceedings in amateur provincial learned societies. He gave the club's president a bald head, spectacles, tights and gaiters. From his description of Mr Pickwick in the first chapter, Seymour was easily able to envisage and draw a thin, learned man. It was Edward Chapman who protested at Seymour's visual conception. 'Good humour and flesh had always gone together since the days of Falstaff', he observed, and he described to Seymour a man he knew at Richmond: 'A fat old beau who would wear, in spite of the ladies' protests, drab tights and black gaiters'. To the satisfaction of publisher and writer alike Seymour created the image of Mr Pickwick we all know today, and this in itself was no doubt a stimulus to Dickens' imagination.

The Posthumous Papers of the Pickwick Club containing a Faithful Record of the Perambulations, Perils, Travels, Adventures and Sporting Transactions of the Corresponding Members, edited by 'Boz' was to be published in monthly parts, as shilling numbers could be expected to reach a wider market than a single expensive volume of sporting plates. The first number, twenty-four pages of letterpress with four illustrations, appeared on 31 March 1836. It was not an immediate success: 400 copies of the first number were sold, but of 1500 copies of the second number sent for distribution in the provinces, only fifty were sold. And there

Right:
Cockney humour was a primary source of Dickens' early art; the comic servants in this print are reminiscent of many of his sharpwitted humourists from Sam Weller onwards.

I say, Sally, wot a good thing it would be if ve vos to jine your £.100
wot the Old Man left yer and the £30 youve got in the Savings Bank &
the £.10 a year wot Missis left yer and them ere 5 Sovereigns wot
young Master guv yer, to my *seven shillings & Sixpence* a veek &
the Christmas Box wot Master's a going to give me ____ve might
then open a Beer shop!

London W Spooner 377 Strand.

had been difficulties behind the scenes. Seymour's initial four plates were cut to three in the second number and subsequently each number contained two illustrations only. Worse still, from Seymour's point of view, the young writer was insisting that he illustrated interpolated 'gothic' tales (stories of melodramatic sensation, pathos and horror, which Dickens happened to have on hand and used to fill up space) quite remote from the normal style and interest of the artist. The publishers supported Dickens, and insisted that Seymour must illustrate his sentimental 'dying clown' tale, which he did. When he had completed the plate, he put a gun in his mouth and blew out his brains. A letter found near his body seemed to hint suspicion of Dickens even while purporting to exonerate him. 'Blame, I charge you, not anyone, it is my own weakness and infirmity', it said, pathetically; but added more doubtfully, 'I don't think anyone has been a malicious enemy to me.'

As the original project had been the monthly issue of plates by Seymour, this unhappy event should have ended *Pickwick*. But Dickens had the bit between his teeth and immediately set about searching for a fresh illustrator. R. W. Buss, a Victorian humorous narrative painter, was tried briefly but found unsatisfactory. The then unknown William Makepeace Thackeray was among the hopeful artists interviewed by Dickens. But the job was given to Hablot Knight Browne, who adopted the *nom de plume* 'Phiz' in imitation of Dickens' 'Boz', and who, proving entirely satisfactory, was to remain Dickens' illustrator for twenty years.

Freed from an unwilling collaborator, Dickens pressed on triumphantly. With the fourth number he introduced Sam Weller, and either the vigour of this character or the fact that four numbers had given the public time to discover this new comic work, led to an amazing upsurge in sales. The *Literary Gazette* found Sam Weller irresistible; new readers began to order back-numbers; and seeing his favourable reviews Dickens felt free to write to his publishers, 'When you have quite done counting the sovereigns, received from *Pickwick*, I should be much obliged to you, to send me up a few.' Chapman and Hall were only too willing. They increased Dickens' fee to twenty-five pounds a month. And still the book's triumph was only beginning: before publication was completed forty thousand copies of each number were being sold, and *Pickwick* was a national craze.

Rich and poor alike delighted in Pickwick. A group of locksmiths, too poor to buy the monthly part even by clubbing together, could nevertheless unite to rent a copy at twopence a day from a circulating library. An invalid receiving spiritual consolation from a clergyman was overheard to murmur, 'Well, thank God, Pickwick will be out in ten days anyway!' Miss Mitford, the author of *Our Village*, wrote to a friend who had not heard of Pickwick: 'I did not think there had been a place where English was spoken to which 'Boz' had not penetrated. All the boys and girls talk his fun—the boys in the streets; and yet they who are of

Even the poor would club together to buy Pickwick. *It was a great deal better than the crude, sensational material offered them in the cheap broadsheets, which gloated over scenes like this one. From Mayhew's* London Labour and the London Poor.

the highest taste like it the most. Sir Benjamin Brodie takes it to read in his carriage between patient and patient; and Lord Denman studies Pickwick on the bench whilst the jury are deliberating.' The commercial possibilities of the name Pickwick were taken up by manufacturers of chintz, cigars, hats, canes, even coats. Hack writers and piratical publishers re-wrote, abridged, adapted, imitated, and vulgarised Pickwick. Curiously, Mr Pickwick himself changed character as he was presented through plagiaristic imitation to the working classes: Dickens' stout, benevolent Quixote was transformed into a bourgeois buffoon, and was presented as a butt rather than a benefactor. But piracy, distortion, and illegal dramatisation could not diminish Dickens' personal triumph. At the age of twenty-five he was the most successful and admired writer of his generation, and already many serious critics realised that the greatest talent since the death of Sir Walter Scott had appeared on the literary scene.

When the publication was completed the young author had received £2,000 for a work which he expected to bring him in less than £400. His publishers had netted £14,000, though this was not as yet a source of exasperation to the young writer.

The accident that Dickens' original commission had been to write text for the monthly issue of plates led him to adopt the practice of writing and publishing his novels in serial form for the rest of his life, and this was imitated by successive Victorian novelists. The robust comedy of goodwill in which lively caricatures enjoyed orgies of food and drink and farcical adventures remained in the mind of the public the Dickensian mode. The respectability of the novel, established by the antiquarian gentleman of letters, Sir Walter Scott, was now to be exploited by a professional writer with lower middle class tastes who had learnt his trade through journalism.

Dickens placing his first literary contribution in the editor's box.

The Writer as Theatregoer

As clerk, as shorthand writer, as journalist, and as successful author, Dickens spent as much of his income as he could on visits to places of public entertainment like the popular pleasure-gardens on the South bank of the Thames, Vauxhall and Cremorne, where open-air concerts and amusements were presented. He had seriously considered a theatrical career for himself, and the writings of his early years show a marked leaning towards the theatre: many of the *Sketches* discuss theatres and popular entertainments; he had three pieces performed on the stage before he realised that he was better suited to writing prose fiction; he was the obvious writer to edit the memoirs of the great clown Grimaldi. Today we tend to see the theatre which so excited Dickens as very second rate. The early nineteenth century was dominated by the absurd distinction between Legitimate and Illegitimate Drama. This rested on the anachronistic grant of licences to perform drama to the two so-called patent companies. But London now had a large population and many more than two or three theatres could find ready audiences. Minor theatre managers were therefore at pains to find forms of entertainment which could not be said to infringe the patent companies' exclusive right to perform drama. The patent companies for their part were deeply concerned to maintain their serious standing as highbrow performers of the classics. Ludicrous agreements as to the bounds of legitimate and illegitimate drama were the result: it was agreed that any play running to five acts was *ipso facto* legitimate. Shorter plays without the addition of music were also legitimate. But what constituted the addition of music? A minimum of five songs to each act was the original requirement; this gradually reduced to five songs over the course of the whole play; and ultimately a single piano tinkling appropriate

mood music at points of high tension or sweet romance might be taken to prove that a melodrama was not a tragedy. In addition, the minor theatre proprietors were free to exploit the public's taste for performing animals, pantomimes, and variety entertainers. Melodrama was the illegitimate substitute for tragedy. Sensational plots were used, often centring on notorious murders. Villains exulted in their wickedness and gloated over their victims; heroines were sugar-sweet and helpless; heroes were strong, clean-limbed and patriotic. Evil was punished, preferably by being led cursing to the gallows. Virtue was rewarded in the reunion of poor but honest lovers, and sometimes with public praise from a vague national dignitary. Crude verse and passages of prose which slipped unwittingly into blank verse provided the style of the dialogue. When Pip in *Great Expectations* went to see Mr Wopsle act, he saw a typical drama for the poor. A handsome boatswain with very tight trousers was the hero, and filled every glass:

A certain dark-complexioned Swab, however, who wouldn't fill, or do anything else that was proposed to him, and whose heart was openly stated (by the boatswain) to be as black as his figurehead, proposed to two other Swabs to get all mankind into difficulties; which was so effectively done (the Swab family having considerable political influence) that it took half the evening to set things right, and then it was only brought about through an honest little grocer with a white hat, black gaiters, and red nose, getting into a clock, with a gridiron, and listening, and coming out, and knocking everybody down from behind with the gridiron whom he couldn't confute with what he'd overheard. This led to Mr Wopsle's (who had never been heard of before) coming in with a star and garter on, as a plenipotentiary of great power direct from the Admiralty, to say that the Swabs were all to go to prison on the spot, and that he had brought the boatswain down the Union Jack, as a slight acknowledgement of his public services.

Audiences in the small, smoky theatres (which were dangerous fire hazards until gas-lighting replaced flaring lime-lights in the mid-century) were rowdy and critical. They hissed and booed villains, and cheered their downfall. If they observed unconvincing acting, or the reappearance of familiar faces in new roles, they would shower the stage with orange peel. The worst hazard the incompetent actor faced was a shower of pennies, thrown to injure rather than reward.

Dickens was no highbrow, and hugely enjoyed the illegitimate drama. In his introduction to Grimaldi's *Memoirs* he spoke of 'the delights—the ten thousand million delights of a pantomime'. He had, he said, 'a strong veneration for clowns', and exclaimed, 'How often have we wished that the Pantaloon were our god-father! And how often thought that to marry a Columbine would be to attain the highest pitch of all human felicity!'

Astley's Amphitheatre, a remarkable combination of circus and theatre, received a section to itself in the *Sketches* and was attended by Kit Nubbles and his family in the *Old Curiosity Shop* and by Mr George in *Bleak House*. Spectacular musical melodramas with huge casts and equestrian interludes were enacted at Astley's, and it is surprising to recall that its vigorous florid vulgarity may have been enjoyed by Jane Austen, as she uses a visit to Astley's to reunite Harriet Smith and Robert Martin in *Emma*. But she never expresses Dickens' enthusiasm for 'all the paint, gilding and looking-glass, the vague smell of horses suggestive of coming wonders, the clean white saw-dust down in the circus, the company coming in and taking their places, the fiddlers looking carelessly up at them while they tuned their instruments, as if they didn't want the play to begin, and knew it all beforehand!'

Mr Crummels the actor's daughter, the Infant Phenomenon in *Nicholas Nickleby*, recalls an absurd fashion of the early years of the century following the triumphs of Master Betty the boy actor. There were twenty or thirty *young wonders*, or *infant prodigies* to be seen between 1802 and 1805: an Infant Billington, an Infant Columbine, a Young Orpheus, an Infant Vestris, an Infant Clown, an Infant Degville, an Ormskirk Roscius and a Comic Roscius, an Infant Hercules, and an Infant Candle-snuffer, being among the most spectacular. An unfortunate Miss Mudie was

Right, above:
'Joey' Grimaldi, the great clown, had his memoirs edited by Dickens.

Right:
A Punch and Judy show. From a painting by A. Boyd Houghton.

Theatre Royal, Adelphi.

The Public is most respectfully informed, that

Mr. MATHEWS

WILL BE

AT HOME!

THIS EVENING,

When he will have the honor to present an ENTIRELY NEW ENTERTAINMENT, in THREE PARTS, entitled

MATHEWS's

Comic Annual

FOR 1830.

With humorous CUTS and other Embellishments!

Published this Day, (Boards), Adelphi, Strand.   (Packed in Boxes), Four Shillings.

PART I.

CHAPTER I.—Reasons for undertaking the Editorship—Parting with Partner—Mrs. Neverend.
CHAPTER II.—Mr. John Downright Shearman, retired Master Tailor—Monsieur Vindrine—Mike Earwig, a Whispering Waiter—British Justice—Police Office—a Skip.

Song, "ZOOLOGICAL GARDENS."

CHAPTER III—Embellishment—Portrait of Mr. Sadjolly, a hale Valetudinarian—his Sons, Master Dickey Sadjolly, and Master Jeremiah Crackthorpe Sadjolly—Youthful Rivalry—turn over a New Leaf to
CHAPTER IV.—Mr. Shakely—Nerves —

Song, "The Cork-Cutters' Festival."

Second Embellishment—Mr. Dispepy's—Double bedded Room—Living Nightmare—Pie-Crust—" What can possibly keep me Awake?

PART II.

CHAPTER I.—Embellishment—Mr. Lavolta—Habitual Risibility—Mr. Sadjolly's Trip to London—Affection of the Spine—Visit to Mr. Polish, the Dentist—the two Boys' Teeth—Mr. Lavolta, with a laughable Tooth-Ache—Jerimiah and Dickiy at School—Invitation to a Public Day—Greek, French, and English Speeches—

Song, "SCHOOL ORATORS."

CHAPTER II—Monsieur Vindrine—Lost Snuff Box—Les Becassines—French Sense of Honour.
CHAPTER III—Lieutenant M'Craw—West Indies—" Honourable Kingston Native and Creole Assembly"—Digression—

Song, "IRISH BERRIN"

CHAPTER IV—Mr. Dispepys' Encore—the Herefordshire Prize Ox, 4684lbs. 10oz.—Raffle—How to Win a great Loss—Mrs. Neverend's last Words—

Song, "VAUXHALL GARDENS."

Mr. MATHEWS' Reading, and Introduction to the Afterpiece.

FINALE.

Mr. Sadjolly---Mr. Lavolta---the Boys- -Vindrine---Earwig---Mr. Mathews.

PART III. Will be presented, as a

PICTORIAL EMBELLISHMENT to the COMIC ANNUAL,

A MONOPOLOLOGUE, to be called

THE LONE HOUSE!

Scene by Messrs. TOMKINS and PITT.—Dresses, by Mr. GODBER & Miss CHERRY.—Properties & Decorations, by Mr. FOSTER.

DRAMATIS PERSONÆ, ENACTED BY MR. MATHEWS.

Mrs. DORA DUNBIRD,   (Deaf Housekeeper).

ANDREW,

(Butler, Groom, Gardener, Cook, to Sir Chevy Melton, when the respective Servants are absent.)
JEREMIAH ABERSHAW, Esq.   -   -   (Prior to his Elevation).
JOHN SHEPHARD, Esq. -   -   -   -   (Antecedent to his Suspension).

DRAMATIS PERSONÆ, REPRESENTED BY ANDREW.

AP LEEKS,   -   -   -   (Sir Chevy Melton's Welsh Gardener).
BECHAMEL,   (Sir Chevy Melton's French Cook).
CAPTAIN GRAPNELL, R.N.   (Friend of Sir Chevy Melton).

BOXES, 4s.—PIT 2s.—GALLERY 1s.—Doors open at half-past Seven, commence at Eight.——☞ NO HALF-PRICE.
BOX OFFICE open from 10 till 4, where PLACES may be taken, and a PRIVATE BOX had Nightly of Mr. CAMPBELL.
PRIVATE BOXES may be had at Mr. Sam's Library, Pall Mall,—Mr. Ebers' Library, Old Bond-St.—Mr. Andrews' New Bond-St.
☞ It is respectfully announced that Places in the Dress Circle cannot be kept unless Tickets are taken when booked.
No Money returned.   Printed by H. Robertson, Cross Court, Russell Court, Drury Lane.

laughed off the stage in 1805, so absurd did it seem that she should present herself as the wife and mistress of adult actors at the age of eight.

But the performer Dickens most enjoyed and whose seasons he visited regularly after 1828 was Charles Mathews the elder. Mathews gave solo performances which he called *At Homes*. He would open with a comic lecture, intersperse comic songs throughout the evening, and deliver varied monologues in different personae. To end his evening he performed what he called a 'monopolylogue', a short one-act play in which by the use of quick changes and quick exits Mathews would play all five or six parts. To differentiate his monologue characters, Mathews developed the use of catch phrases and easily recognisable speech mannerisms. Thus his Commodore Cosmogony relates:

Seen the River Nile, if you mean that—something like a river—thousand miles long—swam down it many a time—eat part of a crocodile there, that wanted to eat me—saw him cry with vexation as I killed him—tears as big as marrow-fat peas—bottled one of them, for the curiosity of the thing.

We are near to the Commodore when we hear Dickens' mad gentleman in *Nicholas Nickleby*:

Tears! Catch the crystal globules—catch 'em—bottle 'em up—cork 'em tight—put sealing wax on the top—seal 'em with a Cupid—label 'em "Best Quality"—and stow 'em away in the fourteen binn, with a bar of iron on top to keep the thunder off.

For Dickens wrote as a theatre-goer, and loved to compose, as Ruskin said, 'with a circle of stage fire'. In later life his daughter observed that when he was writing he would frequently leap up from his desk, run to a mirror, and mouth sentences into it as if he were acting the part he was writing. With phrases or sentences of different length recurring, one can observe the Mathews' technique, in essentials, appearing as late as Flora Finching in *Little Dorrit*.

If, for our taste, Dickens' serious moments are too crudely melodramatic, we are appropriately compensated by the rich entertainment from the comic illegitimate drama which he has preserved for us. The theatre in turn has borrowed his plots and characters, from his day, when pirates exasperated him by dramatising serial novels he had not completed, to our own, when films and television have joined the hunt.

Left:
A playbill for Mathews' performance.

Right, above:
Charles Mathews was Dickens, favourite actor. His At Homes were solo performances culminating in short plays in which, as this print shows, he played all the parts.

Astley's amphitheatre was stage and circus ring combined. Dickens loved its vigorous entertainment, which even the lady-like Jane Austen had enjoyed.

'Dearest Darling Pig'

How little the general public knew of Charles Dickens at the outset of his career! When *Pickwick* and *Oliver Twist*, which were appearing simultaneously, both ceased publication for two months in 1837, with the explanation that a domestic tragedy made it impossible for the author to continue writing immediately, rumours flew around. It was all a hoax! Boz was a young genius of eighteen, whose overwork at the behest of unscrupulous publishers had led to a brain storm or his sudden demise! Boz had turned Roman Catholic and abandoned fiction! Boz was a syndicate, now broken up! There would be no more Boz!

In fact, to his friends and intimates, Boz was known as a contented young married man, who, by 1837, was the father of the richly named infant Charles Culliford Boz Dickens—the Boz being included because impetuous John Dickens had blurted it out at the christening. It was while he was a reporter on the *Morning Chronicle* that Dickens met Catherine Hogarth, eldest daughter of the *Evening Chronicle*'s Scottish editor. Slow, placid, sulky, and perhaps something of a depressive personality, she was utterly different from the pert Maria Beadnell. Even in looks she differed: where Maria had been small and finely drawn, Kate was more voluptuously built, with sleepy lidded eyes, and full breasts.

George Hogarth was only too willing to accept his lively colleague as a son-in-law, and in 1835 the young couple were engaged. Accepting the young Charles Dickens as a prospective son-in-law was a bit like inviting a whirlwind into the house. The Hogarth family were sitting together after dinner one night, when a sailor burst in through the French windows, danced a quick hornpipe to the accompaniment of his own whistling, and ducked out into the garden again. A few minutes later the doorbell rang, and Charles

strolled in, looking perfectly composed: he had borrowed the nautical costume to play the joke.

With Kate, Dickens was not going to be the sport of a wilful child. From the outset of their engagement his letters to her are filled with severe and almost paternal reproof and admonishment. At times he seems to be addressing a memory of Maria rather than Kate:

If a feeling of you know what—a capricious restlessness of you can't tell what, and a desire to tease, you don't know why, give rise to it—overcome it; it will never make you more amiable, I more fond, or either of us more happy. If three weeks or three months of my society has wearied you, do not trifle with me, using me like any other toy that suits your humour for the moment; but make the acknowledgement to me frankly at once—I shall not forget you lightly, but you will need no second warning.

As the engagement developed Kate's lover treated her sulks less and less as manifestations of adult behaviour. He would explain patiently that pressure of work inevitably kept him away from her, but approach her own indignation with the coy query, 'Not coss?' It was of a part with his affectionate nicknames for her: she was his 'own dearest darling Pig', his 'dearest Wig',

Right, above:
Charles Dickens, aged eighteen, painted by his aunt Janet Barrow.

Right:
The Nickleby portrait, painted to celebrate the completion of Nicholas Nickleby. *Dickens' friends agreed that this picture, more than any other, captured his essential liveliness and energy.*

his 'Mouse', or 'Titmouse' or in baby talk 'Tatie'.

But the apparent childishness of Catherine was no bar to marriage in Dickens' eyes. The women who meant most to him were rarely highly educated or markedly intelligent. Preparations went forward, with Dickens buying jugs, decanters and jars, and sending to Scotland for the special toddy-kettle which Kate demanded. The acceptance of *Pickwick* offered a degree of financial security, and in March of 1836 the young couple were quietly married and went for one week's honeymoon—it was all the vacation work allowed him to take—at the village of Chalk in Kent. On their return they moved into Dickens' chambers in Furnivall's Inn where they were joined by Kate's devoted sixteen-year-old sister Mary. It is Mary, in her schoolgirl's grammar, who gives us our most intimate glimpse of the young couple :

> 'I have just returned home from spending a most delightfully happy month with dearest Catherine in her own house ! I only wish you could see her in it, and sincerely hope you may some day or other, not far distant, she makes a most capital housekeeper and is as happy as the day is long—I think they are more devoted than ever since their Marriage if that be possible—I am sure you would be delighted with him if you knew him he is such a nice creature and so clever he is courted and made up to by all the literary Gentlemen, and has more to do in that way as he can well manage.

In view of Dickens' later complaints it is interesting to note that Catherine once appeared a 'most capital

Above :
Miniature of Kate Dickens.
Right :
Dickens with Kate and Mary.

35

housekeeper'. Nor is there any questionable excess of affection in Mary's girlish enthusiasm for her brother-in-law. The *mènage à trois* was entirely successful, and when the birth of Charles junior made the set of rooms inconveniently cramped for the household, Mary moved with them to the new house Dickens leased in Doughty Street, Holborn.

48 Doughty Street is now the headquarters of the Dickens Fellowship. But the young family who moved in at the end of March in 1837 were not taking up residence in a historical monument. Doughty Street was then a new private road, with porters in mulberry coloured liveries manning the gates at each end. Here the Dickenses expected to pass a long and happy period of their lives. Alas, their perfect happiness in their new home was to last no more than a month.

Left, above:
Cremorne Gardens, the popular pleasure gardens Dickens frequently visited. From a painting by Phoebus Levin.

Left, below:
Buckingham St, Strand, painted by E. J. Niemann, 1854. The old Hungerford footbridge is in the background.

Above:
Cottage at Chalk, Kent, reputed to be the 'umble 'ome of Uriah Heep, where Dickens may have spent his honeymoon.

Right:
Front door of 48 Doughty St, the house Dickens moved into after the success of Pickwick.

'Young, Beautiful and Good'

There is little worthy of record in the life of Mary Scott Hogarth. She loved her elder sister Catherine, she admired her successful brother-in-law Charles, she stayed with them at Furnivall's Inn after their honeymoon, she went with them on a further holiday to Chalk, she moved with them to Doughty Street. And there, at the age of seventeen, she died suddenly and unexpectedly.

It was early in May. Mary had spent two days with her mother at Brompton. On the Saturday when she returned Dickens and Kate took her to the St James' Theatre, where his farce *Is She His Husband?* was shortly to be performed. Theatres in those days usually performed a short curtain raiser and a concluding farce in addition to the main piece of the evening, so that there was nothing unusual in a theatre party reaching home after midnight. It was one o'clock in the morning when the family went to bed in the highest of spirits. Almost the moment Mary entered her bedroom a choking cry was heard, and Dickens, racing to her, saw at once that she was gravely ill. His younger brother Fred, who was also staying at Doughty Street at the time, was sent out for the doctor; Dickens and Kate tried every remedy they could think of; but all was of no avail, and at three o'clock on Sunday afternoon Dickens realised that the body he was supporting on the bed had been lifeless for some time. Heart disease was suspected.

Mary was buried in Kensal Green cemetery with an inscription composed by Dickens on her tombstone:

> Mary Scott Hogarth
> died seventh May 1837
> Young Beautiful and Good,
> God in his mercy
> numbered her with his angels.

His immediate letters to friends followed her death express the general grief of the entire family. 'A sister of Mrs Dickens' a young and lovely girl, who has been the grace and ornament of our home for the whole time of our marriage, died here yesterday.' 'She has been our constant companion since our marriage; the grace and life of our home.—Judge how deeply we feel this fearfully sudden deprivation.' 'She was our constant friend and companion, and the loss independent of its fearful suddenness, is severely felt by us.'

But within a week Mary's (possibly imagined) perfections played a larger part in his mind. To one friend he described her as, 'the dear girl whom I loved, after my wife, more deeply and fervently than anyone on earth'. But to a closer friend he confessed that, 'I solemnly believe that so perfect a creature never breathed. I knew her inmost heart, and her real worth and value. She had not a fault.' By now Mary was apparently giving meaning to Dickens' own existence; he thanked God that she had died in his arms and that her last words had been of him. It would surely have distressed the innocent young girl deeply to have known that she left an idealised image in her brother-in-law's mind which her sister would never to able to live up to. In Dickens' mind Mary would remain a slim sixteen while Kate grew older and stouter. Mary would continue to seem an embodiment of girlish innocence, meekness and purity, while Kate bore the marks of child-bearing on her body and the tone of

Above:
Little Nell, the pathetic heroine in whom Dickens recaptured the personal tragedy of his sister-in-law's early death.
Right:
Mary Hogarth.

Right :
Dickens' taste in women was not outstanding. His sweet-hearts were not overintelligent, and the heroines of his novels are insipid and incredibly virtuous like Dora, the 'child wife' of David Copperfield.
Below :
Dickens sketched by Cruickshank, his first illustrator.

wifely complaint in her voice. Adolescent girls would always seem to Dickens to possess a moral perfection his wife sadly lacked, and this, in the end, was to bring his marriage to scandalous collapse and public separation.

For months Dickens dreamt of Mary every night. There seemed to him something peculiarly private and intimate about these dreams, so that he never revealed them to Kate, until, about a year later, he mentioned them in a letter while he was away from home. Immediately the dreams ceased. He did in later life,

however, have one further memorable dream of Mary. It was while he was staying in Italy. He dreamt of a Madonna-like shape which he immediately knew to be Mary's. He reached out towards it and asked it for some proof of the visitation. Was the Roman Catholic religion the best, he wondered? 'For *you*', answered Mary's spirit, 'it is the best.' Dickens woke up with tears running down his face. He was a profound anti-Catholic, whose English Protestantism was grossly offended by the church in Italy; the 'spirit's' message was not one he could take seriously. Yet it never occurred to him to doubt the emotional importance of the dream for himself.

The immediate effect of the bereavement on his work was that he stopped writing *Pickwick* and *Oliver* for two months–the only occasion in his career on which he disappointed his public. A further effect was revealed in *Oliver Twist*. The development of the plot had suggested that Rose Mayly would die to give a lachrymose touch to the conclusion. In the event, Dickens found himself unable to kill off a character so powerfully reminiscent of Mary.

The long term effect was more important. The death of innocent youth would always appear to Dickens the most profoundly tragic note in the artist's register. Smike, Little Nell, Paul Dombey, and Joe the Crossing-Sweeper are all descendants of the Mary Hogarth who lived in Dickens' mind. They are dragged through lugubrious deathbed scenes in which they foresee Heaven: Smike, for example, 'spoke of beautiful gardens, which he said stretched out before him, and were filled with figures of men, women, and many children, all with light upon their faces; then, whispered that it was Eden–and so died'. These noble deaths after their virtuous (if brief) lives are morally uplifting for both readers and adult characters in the books. Yet the childish virtues the characters have exhibited seem very passive: very much a matter of never saying or doing a wrong thing in spite of intolerable stresses. Mary Hogarth, after all, had not had an eventful life, She was evidently quite pleasant to have around the house. But as a model for childish saints, she was a little static. And much of our exasperation with Dickens' dying children springs from his practice of telling us how *good* they are, without ever showing them enacting heroic virtue.

Even the heroines who do not suffer lingering deaths and a slow passage into the care of the angels at Dickens' authorial hands are touched with the spirit of Mary Hogarth. The passive and somewhat insipid virtues of good young women in the novels are Dickens' tribute to the lost sister-in-law whose ring he wore until he died, and by whose side he hoped to be buried himself. Later experience never cured Dickens of the belief that the good die young. He was subsequently to remark of a young girl whose shy modesty caught his attention at a public recital that she could not have long to live, and the fact that he watched her outlive his interest in her in no way led him to change his general opinion.

Mr Popular Sentiment

For many readers Dickens is first and foremost the great humanitarian and social reformer. It is a reputation he deserves. No previous novelist had made such full and varied use of the form to attack specific social abuses and make inhumanity appear ridiculous.

It is in some ways remarkable that we should all remember how Oliver Twist asked for more, when the book contains so many more striking highlights: Fagin, teaching his boys to steal; the liveliness of the Artful Dodger; Sykes on the run and Fagin in the condemned cell. But Dickens' sub-title, *The Parish-Boy's Progress*, shows that we have remembered what he intended us to remember. In 1834 Parliament had introduced the new Poor Law. Well-meaning economists feared that the distribution of cash benefits to the poor might encourage people to live on the dole. Equally, they might be 'pauperised' if workhouse accommodation was more comfortable than the slums outside. So the supplementing of wages from parish rates was ended, and the workhouse regime was tightened up. The country at large recognised this as punishing people who had committed no crime. But only Dickens was able to turn indignation to mirth, and make the 'sage, deep, philosophical men' behind the new Poor Law look silly as well as hardhearted:

When they came to turn their attention to the workhouse, they found out at once, what ordinary folks would never have discovered—the poor people liked it! It was a regular place of public entertainment for the poorer classes; a tavern where there was nothing to pay; a public breakfast, dinner, tea, and supper all the year round; a brick-and-mortar elysium, where it was all play and no work. "Oh Ho!" said the Board looking very knowing; "we are the fellows to set this to rights; we'll stop it all, in

no time." So, they established the rule, that all poor people should have the alternative (for they would compel nobody, not they), of being starved by a gradual process in the house, or by a quick one out of it. With this view, they contracted with the water-works to lay on an unlimited supply of water; and with a corn-factor to supply periodically small quantities of oatmeal; and issued three meals of thin gruel a day, with an onion twice a week, and half a roll on Sundays . . . The relief was inseparable from the workhouse and the gruel; and that frightened people.

Although he contributed to the public hatred of workhouses, Dickens did not live to see them close. But his next campaign succeeded within his own lifetime. With *Oliver Twist* out of the way, he was searching for the subject of a new novel. A childhood friend who had been at a private boarding school in Yorkshire came into his mind, and he said, 'I was always curious about Yorkshire schools—fell, long afterwards and at sundry times, into the way of hearing more about them—at last, having an audience, resolved to write about them.'

Private boarding schools in the North Riding of Yorkshire were cheap, distant from London, and in many cases were little more than boy-farms. Many of them advertised 'no vacations' as one of their main attractions. Lazy and selfish parents, or the parents of unwanted illegitimate children, could legally put them out of sight and out of mind by sending them away to school in Yorkshire. Low fees—possibly as little as sixteen pounds a year, all found—and fulsome advertisements in the London newspapers might mislead gullible parents of limited means into believing that they were buying the best education they could afford for their children by sending them to school in Yorkshire.

A certain notoriety attached to the Yorkshire schools when they attracted Dickens' attention. In February 1838 he made a flying trip to Yorkshire taking his illustrator, Hablot Knight Browne, to see what they were really like. A chance fellow traveller in the coach to Grantham turned out to be the mistress of a Yorkshire school returning from her holiday in London. 'She was a very queer old body', said Dickens, 'and shewed us a long letter she was carrying to one of the boys from his father, containing a severe lecture (enforced and aided by many texts from the scripture) *on his refusing to eat boiled meat.* She was very communicative, drank a great deal of brandy and water, and towards evening became insensible, in which state we left her.' She evidently provided data for Squeers, bringing his boys messages from London:

"Mobbs's mother-in-law," said Squeers, "took to her bed on hearing that he wouldn't eat fat, and has been very ill ever since. She wishes to know, by an early post, where he expects to go to, if he quarrels with his vittles; and with what feelings he could turn up his nose at the cow's liver broth, after his good master had asked a blessing on it. This was told her in the London newspapers—not by Mr Squeers, for he is too kind and too good to set anybody against anybody—and it has vexed her so much, Mobbs can't think. She is sorry to find he is discontented, which is sinful and horrid, and hopes Mr Squeers will flog him into a happier state of mind."

Incidentally, Dickens appears to have slipped himself and Browne into *Nicholas Nickleby*, as 'two of the front outside passengers' who broke the journey at Grantham.

In Yorkshire, the pair pretended to be looking for a school for the son of a widowed friend. The schoolmasters were suspicious of them, and showed them little; but a lawyer in Barnard Castle secretively urged them not to let a child into the hands of the 'scoundrels' while there was 'a horse to hold in all London, or a gutter to lie asleep in!' Satisfied that cruelty and negligence were being practised in the schools he had seen, Dickens returned south, stopping at York to visit the Minster and admire the superb Five Sisters window.

Browne had not been idle. His drawings of Wackford Squeers were recognisable as caricatures of William Shaw, the headmaster of Bowes Academy. Shaw had been compelled to pay £500 damages in an action brought against him by two parents whose children lost their eyesight through his negligence. His ignorance and severity were unremarkable in the district, but as his acquaintances observed, he was the only Yorkshire schoolmaster who had one eye, 'and the popular prejudice runs in favour of two'. Shaw was ruined by *Nicholas Nickleby*, and the wide publicity Dotheboys Hall gave to Yorkshire education

Squeers thrashed by Nicholas : a recognisable caricature of Yorkshire schoolmaster William Shaw. Illustration from Nicholas Nickleby.

helped put a stop to this disgraceful exploitation of children.

In calling Dickens 'Mr Popular Sentiment', Anthony Trollope rightly directed attention to the fact that Dickens tended to take up well established causes rather than discovering previously unobserved abuses. But the implied smear is unjust: Dickens personally investigated and seriously examined the institutions he attacked, and although he was willing to shed an easy tear in describing the victims' plight, he achieved his strongest effects by vigorous satirical comedy. While he hated the cruelty to children which has appeared all too often in England, he made its practitioners memorable boobies and comic villains. Mr Bumble's self-importance strikes at the ridiculousness of the tyrannical Jack-in-office; the obscenity of grown men beating children in the name of education is robbed of all dignity when Mr Squeers pompously advertises the teaching of 'singlestick' at his academy.

Tragedy of the True Sort

By the end of 1839 Dickens was ready to move from Doughty Street to a more imposing house. He now had three successful novels behind him and his son, Charles, had been followed by two daughters. Significantly, the first was named after Mary and only the second after Kate.

With a twelve-year lease on Number One Devonshire Terrace, plans for new work could be considered. There was a hindrance to work; Dickens had quarrelled with the publisher Richard Bentley for whom he had edited the monthly *Miscellany*, and for whom he had contracted to write two further novels. Bentley had tried to interfere with the editor's control over the *Miscellany*, and without considerable pressure was unwilling to raise the royalties he had contracted to pay Dickens to match the writer's newly acquired fame and importance. Rather than create novels for the benefit of a man he now regarded as an enemy, Dickens wished to start a new periodical. *Master Humphrey's Clock* was to come out weekly, and contain short stories from among the manuscripts owned by an eccentric old recluse.

When he finally brought out the first number, 70,000 copies were sold, and Dickens was delighted with the success of the new venture. It was to be shortlived. The public had assumed that this was a new novel by Charles Dickens, and finding it to be

Above:
Little Nell sent the Victorian reading public into floods of tears. Illustration by Dalziel from a later edition of the book.
Left:
Great Ormond St children's hospital. Dickens was very fond of children and this was one of his favourite charities.

merely a miscellany, stopped buying it. Sales fell away in the second number and by the third it seemed that Dickens had his first outright failure on his hands. To rescue his investment he turned a short story into a long serial. It was to prove one of the major triumphs of his career. For old Master Humphrey, on a midnight ramble, had encountered a little girl who lived with her grandfather at a dusty old antique shop. *The Old Curiosity Shop*, with its child heroine Nell, arose from the ashes of *Master Humphrey's Clock*.

The death of Little Nell has become a byword for tasteless tear-jerking: 'Why dost thou lie so idle there, dear Nell . . . when there are bright red berries out of doors waiting for thee to pluck them? Why dost thou lie so idle there, when thy little friends come creeping to the door, crying "where is Nell—sweet Nell?"– and sob, and weep, because they do not see thee.' And so it goes on, page after page. Yet in its own day, serious and learned critics regarded it as profoundly moving tragedy. Dickens himself regarded it as one of his finest pieces of work; it would have amazed him to know that it could fall into disesteem while other areas of his writing continued to be highly valued. The pathetic death of an innocent child was an effect he attempted again with Paul Dombey, and eminent Victorian after eminent Victorian testifies to the tragic worth of these scenes in the nineteenth century.

In the early years of the century, while he was editor of the *Edinburgh Review*, Lord Jeffrey had been a severe critic with no nonsense about him: he once opened a review of Wordsworth with the exclamation, 'This will never do!' But Dickens' dying children utterly conquered him in his retirement. A friend found him weeping in his library and asked whether anyone had died. 'Yes, indeed', he replied, 'I'm a great goose to have given way so, but I couldn't help it.

Right, below:
A begging baby sitter from St. Giles, who guarded the children of the poor while their mothers worked. Taken later in the century, the photograph shows how little conditions changed during this period.

Below:
Boy crossing sweepers, from Mayhew's London Labour and the London Poor. *Little Nell's admirers saw nothing extraordinary in the real-life misery that confronted them everyday.*

You'll be sorry to hear that Little Nellie, Boz's Little Nellie, is dead.' After Paul Dombey's death he wrote to Dickens, 'O, my dear Dickens! What a no. 5 you have now given us! I cried and sobbed over it last night. Since that divine Nellie was found dead on her humble couch there has been nothing like the actual dying of that sweet Paul.' Little Tiny Tim in *A Christmas Carol* he also found, 'almost as sweet and touching as Nellie'.

Daniel O'Connell, the Irish Nationalist M.P., read of Nell's death in a railway train. He burst into tears, cried out, 'He should not have killed her', and threw the book out of the carriage window. Thomas Carlyle, dourest of Victorian sages, who was inclined to despise mere fiction-writers, was nevertheless overcome by *The Old Curiosity Shop*. From America, Washington Irving praised Nell's 'exquisite pathos' and 'moral sublimity'. American readers had to wait for each number to come across the Atlantic: as the story neared its completion, a crowd at New York pier shouted to an incoming vessel, 'Is Little Nell dead?'

Dickens was as deeply moved as his readers. 'I am breaking my heart over this story', he told the illustrator of *The Old Curiosity Shop*, and as readers' letters poured in, begging him to spare Nell's life, he found it difficult to proceed with the book and repeatedly found excuses not to return to his desk. When he had finished it, he wrote, 'I am the wretchedest of the wretched. It casts the most horrible shadow upon me, and it is as much as I can do to keep moving at all.' His purpose had been humane and compassionate: 'When I first began to keep my thoughts upon the ending of the tale, I resolved to try and do something which might be read by people about whom Death had been, with a softened feeling, and with consolation.' Among his intimates Dickens was notably successful at comforting the bereaved: William Charles Macready, the great tragic actor, suffered the deepest distress on losing his three-year-old daughter in 1840, but noted in his journal, 'Received a dear and most affectionate note from Dickens which comforted me as much as I can be comforted.' Within a few months Macready was urging Dickens to spare Nell's life, and received a personal note from Dickens with his number of *Master Humphrey's Clock* containing the death of Nell. The scene proved the most painful Macready had ever read.

Bereavement was common in the huge Victorian families with primitive medical attention. The cult of 'sensibility'—the self-conscious attempt to respond with intense feeling to anything remotely pathetic—which since the late eighteenth century had appeared a mark of civilisation, made it unusually painful. Undoubtedly the success of Dickens' pathetic deathbed scenes with his contemporary audience lay in their skilful reawakening of private griefs, and the apparent larger meaning given to such grief by the ascription of moral perfection and a heavenly after-life to the dying children. Yet before the nineteenth century was out, Oscar Wilde had quipped that one must have a heart of stone to read the death of Little Nell without laughing. The impertinent witticism does not explain the failure for us of Dickens' pathos. But from among Dickens' friends, one voice in his own day expressed discriminating disapproval.

'I'm never up to his young girls' said Daniel Maclise, the painter, 'He is so very fond of the age of "Nell", when they are most insipid.' Here, surely, is the heart of the problem. It's not that the children's deaths fail in sadness, but the excessive moral weight Dickens ascribes to their passive personalities which offends us. Little Paul Dombey's catchphrase, 'What are the wild waves saying', proved to Victorian readers that the doomed child had some mystical insight into the truths of life and death. For us the proof is not clear. One remembers how *ordinary* a girl Mary Hogarth, Dickens' model from life of doomed youth, had been. She had done nothing spectacularly virtuous; she had simply been pleasant to have around. But this was not enough for a Victorian moralist, and Dickens had transformed her into a monument of virtue in his own mind. Now, in his novels, he re-created the simplicity and naivety of childhood, and demanded that its extinction at the hands of Death be seen as having a sacrificial or martyr-like value. Bereaved Victorian parents willingly gave the assent which we inevitably refuse.

Friends and Acquaintances

From his father Dickens inherited a sociable nature. John and Charles Dickens both enjoyed mixing a convivial bowl of punch, though neither was a heavy drinker. A jolly dinner at a slightly distant inn–*Jack Straw's Castle* on Hampstead Heath, or *The Star and Garter* at Richmond–was always to Dickens' taste, and his circle of men friends was very important to him.

Two of Dickens' closest friends were notoriously difficult and unpopular personalities. John Forster was literary and dramatic critic on the *Examiner* when Dickens first met him. This was the famous Radical journal in which Leigh Hunt had conducted the attacks upon the Prince Regent, for which he was jailed. It was now under the editorship of Albany Fonblanque, and its favourable review of *Sketches by Boz*, coupled with its political past, endeared it and its contributors to Dickens. But Forster was also becoming recognised as a useful mediator in disputes between literary men and their publishers, and Dickens was first referred to him when he was trying to prevent Macrone from re-issuing the *Sketches* in the green-wrapped format of *Pickwick*. Forster tried to buy back the copyright from Macrone but advised Dickens to refuse the exorbitant price the publisher demanded. Dickens rejected Forster's advice on this occasion, but consulted him on all his publications in the future, and became his most intimate friend.

Forster was the epitome of the Victorian 'buttoned-up man.' He not only fastened all his coat buttons; he had the stiff and dignified self-importance to go with this precision in dress. On holiday with the Dickenses at Broadstairs he seemed to do the ocean a favour by bathing in it. As his career prospered–he was to succeed Fonblanque as editor of the *Examiner*, and later to succeed Dickens as editor of the *Daily News*–his pomposity and tactlessness grew proportionately.

By the eighteen-sixties, when he had married a rich wife, he bullied guests and servants outrageously at his dinner table, and quarrelled jealously with the admiring young men who by then surrounded Dickens. Yet it was cruel of Dickens to caricature his mannerisms in Mr Podsnap, the uncultivated self-satisfied bourgeois boor of *Our Mutual Friend*; Forster was a devoted and loyal friend, and after Dickens' death was at pains to preserve his friend's reputation untarnished.

Their most serious quarrel fell on August 16th, 1841, at dinner, and was observed by William Macready:

Forster . . . waxed warm, and at last some sharp observations led to personal retorts between him and Dickens. He displayed his usual want of tact, and Dickens flew into so violent a passion as quite to forget himself and give Forster to understand that he was in his house which he should be glad if he would leave. Forster behaved very foolishly. I stopped him; spoke to both of them and observed that for an angry instant they were about to destroy a friendship valuable to both . . . . Forster behaved very *weakly*; would not accept the repeated acknowledgement communicated to him that Dickens regretted the passion, etc. But stayed skimbling-skambling a parcel of unmeaning words, and at last finding he could obtain no more, made a sort of speech, accepting what he had before declined. He was silent and not recovered–no wonder!–during the whole evening. Mrs Dickens had gone out in tears. It was a very painful scene.

Right:
John Forster.

Macready, the mediating hero of this 'painful scene', was himself a difficult and prickly character. He was the leading tragic actor of his day; in an ode Tennyson called him 'moral, grave, sublime'. He did much to restore the original texts of Shakespeare to the stage instead of the chopped and altered versions which had been used since the eighteenth century. After the death of Edmund Kean he was the unchallenged star of Covent Garden and Drury Lane. Yet he hated his profession, and was unpopular within it.

Part of his unpopularity was due to one of his merits: he insisted on proper rehearsals, which were regarded by nineteenth-century actors as a waste of time. When Dickens was supervising amateur theatricals in Montreal, he recognised the example he was following: 'Everybody was told they would have to submit to the most iron despotism, and didn't I come Macready over them!' But his snobbish dignity, his wish to be thought of as a gentleman rather than an actor, and his hectoring theatre discipline were more reasonably resented. These, together with his spluttering mannerisms and preference for literary company, were well caught in this comic monologue from a theatre journal, which shows him drilling his company in rehearsal:

> Where is the tailor-man, that head, fool, brute, beast, ass? How dare you annoy me, sir, in this manner? Have you got a soul or sense?... Look, who wrote these calls? Gentlemen, look about you; read for yourselves: here is "Macbeth" spelt "Mackbeth". Who is that talking at the wings? Henry! Henry! go down and tell the stage door-keeper I expect him to go away–to leave the theatre immediately... Mr Forster–Oh, show Mr Forster to my room; no, stop! My dear Dickens, howd'y do? Talfourd! your hand; another and another! Browning! Bulwer! a-a- walk into the green-room!

His greatest stage success was as Macbeth, but even here he made himself a bad reputation in the profession. In his stage fights, he attacked his opponents with such ferocity that it was physically dangerous to play Macduff to Macready's Macbeth. On the other hand, let an actor bump into Macready accidentally onstage, and a torrent of oaths would greet him. The audience must have been amused on the night when Macready was lying on stage, supposedly dead, and a nervous young actor trod on his hand. Like a shot, the corpse sat up and moaned, 'Beast! Beast of hell!'– and then subsided again.

Left, above:
W. C. Macready.

Augustus Egg.
Right:
George Cruickshank, the first illustrator of Dickens' books

For all his faults, Macready was a deeply sensitive man and Dickens valued his friendship. When he and Kate went to America, it was with the Macreadys that they left their children, though the chilly severity of the Macready household was hated by the infants Charley, Mamie, and Katey. Their pet raven, Grip, was probably left with another friend, the animal painter Edwin Landseer.

Several painters were included in Dickens' circle of friends, chief among them, Daniel Maclise. Dickens found him a wayward, delightful fellow, and enjoyed his company on holidays, where Maclise's sunny disposition, love of leisure, and serene imperturbability in the face of mishaps made him an invaluable friend. Maclise painted and drew many of the literary men of his generation, and the portrait of Dickens, now in the National Portrait Gallery, which he painted to celebrate the completion of *Nicholas Nickleby*, was regarded by those who knew him as an impeccable likeness, bringing out the animation and vitality of his face.

Two more painters on easy terms with Dickens were Clarkson Stanfield and Augustus Egg. Stanfield was a theatrical scene-painter, whose help was to prove a great asset when Dickens began to take amateur theatricals seriously. Augustus Egg, the charming Victorian narrative painter, hoped to marry Dickens' sister-in-law Georgina. He failed, as she had no wish to leave her brother-in-law's household, but he has left us with vivid impressions of her youthful attraction. The beard Dickens grew in later life was intended to put to shame the sparse hairs which Egg had fancifully allowed to grow on his chin.

Inevitably, Dickens was associating with many journalists. The early contributors to *Punch* shared his undogmatic radicalism and heated opposition to Protectionist Toryism, and *Punch*'s first editor, Mark Lemon, was to the Dickens children their beloved 'Uncle Porpoise'. Douglas Jerrold, another early *Punch* man, was an old friend whose widow and children received help from Dickens after his death. *Punch*'s most distinguished contributor, William Makepeace Thackeray, was a friend, but never really close ; Thackeray was always too much aware of his own rivalry with Dickens for the public's favour, and had never really shared the Radicalism of his colleagues on *Punch*. It was no surprise that the uneasy relationship of the two novelists should culminate in a public quarrel.

Two friends from the days before Dickens' fame were brought by him into more distinguished circles : Thomas Mitton had been a fellow clerk at Ellis and Blackmore's ; and Thomas Beard had brought Dickens onto the *Morning Chronicle* where he was himself a reporter. Beard outlived Dickens, and earned for himself the name of 'Dickens' earliest friend'.

There was an ever-widening circle of literary and social celebrities who had a greater or lesser acquaintance with Dickens. Edward Bulwer had been the public's favourite novelist before *Pickwick*. He later changed his name, and is better known as Bulwer

Clarkson Stanfield.

Alfred, Lord Tennyson.

Lytton (Thackeray mocked at the resounding collection of names he sported before his death: Edward George Earle Lytton Bulwer Lytton, Lord Lytton). Bulwer was generously free from jealousy of his rival's success, and he, Ainsworth, Disraeli and Dickens were the noted young dandy novelists of the eighteen-thirties. Leader of dandyism was Count Alfred D'Orsay, who lived scandalously at Gore House, Kensington, with his sister-in-law, Lady Blessington. When Lady Blessington was left a widow, with her husband's estate entailed to her thirteen-year-old stepdaughter, D'Orsay had married the little girl and gained control of her money. He now ignored his wife, while he and Lady Blessington squandered her money and entertained literary men in London.

A more respectable acquaintance for Dickens was Samuel Rogers, the old banker poet, who gave literary breakfasts, and watched the decline of literary taste as sadly as his juniors watched the decline of his amiable person.

Thomas Talfourd was a closer friend: Dickens dedicated *Pickwick* to him, and based David Copperfield's friend Tommy Traddles on this literary lawyer. Talfourd was the author of some frigid poetic dramas, of which the best known was *Ion*. This ultimately drew from Dickens one of his most atrocious puns, when he entitled a dummy book '*Steele* by the author of *Ion*'.

There were more casual acquaintances, whose position at the centre of the literary scene nonetheless made Dickens proud to call them friends: Alfred Tennyson, the rising poet; Thomas Carlyle, philosopher and historian, who looked down on Dickens as a mere entertainer, but sent him a cartload of books on the French revolution to help him with *A Tale of Two Cities*; feckless Leigh Hunt and leonine Walter Savage Landor, men of letters who were to be indignant when Dickens caricatured them in *Bleak House* as Harold Skimpole and Lawrence Boythorn. All these might claim friendship with the young man whose long curly brown hair, brilliant waistcoats, and elaborately pinned cravats made his appearance striking.

With the younger members of the circle, Dickens went for long, vigorous walks, or rode into the country, and indulged his taste for outrageous puns and elaborate horseplay. (When Queen Victoria married, for example, he and Maclise pretended to be dying for love of her and to resent Prince Albert deeply. A young lady at Broadstairs was distressed when Dickens jokingly professed a passion for her, and held her under the pier while the tide came in, ruining her dress). More staid friends might enjoy the dinners Dickens hospitably dispensed, with too much of everything—food, flowers and fruit. Friends' children adored him: he was a fine amateur conjurer, and organised children's amusements with great gusto. Only the most perceptive observed that his own family seemed slightly in awe of him, and were more relaxed when his buoyant, boisterous presence was removed.

John Leech.
Daniel Maclise.

America

'After balancing, considering, and weighing the matter in every point of view, I have made up my mind (with God's leave) to go to America—and to start as soon after Christmas as it will be safe to go', said Dickens.

'Aren't there disagreeable enough people to describe in Blackburn and Leeds?' enquired Albany Fonblanque; and Lady Holland, the society hostess, added, 'Why cannot you go down to Bristol and see some of the third and fourth class people there and they'll do just as well?'

But Dickens was determined to go and see for himself the democratic republic which appealed to his radical outlook, and on his return, to write a travel book which should put America's case before Europe with greater sympathy than had hitherto been done. Accordingly, he and Kate had new wardrobes made, and arranged their itinerary. Maclise painted the children with Grip the raven, and it was some comfort to Kate in her absence from them to have this painting always open on her dressing table. On 4 January 1842, Dickens and Kate went to Liverpool and boarded the *Britannia*, the first Cunard steamer to deliver the Atlantic mails.

Steamer travel was a slightly alarming novelty in the 1840s. At first, Dickens was amused by its inconvenience; in his tiny stateroom he announced that what the stewards called his bed must surely be a muffin beaten flat. But by the time the Atlantic had been crossed, alarm at the prospect of losing the funnel in a storm had persuaded Dickens that he must return by sail.

In Boston the newspaper reporters came leaping aboard the *Britannia* to interview the distinguished visitor. Dickens was by now something of a metropolitan dandy, and the grubby provincialism of American newspaper men seemed to him to do the

Charley, Mamie, Katey and Wally with Grip the raven, painted by Maclise. This is the picture the Dickenses took with them to America.

Right, above:
The Britannia, *Cunard's first steamer, in Boston harbour. Dickens sailed on her in 1842.*

Far right:
Washington Irving.

Right:
Charles Dana.

profession no credit. Indeed, the lionisation he was to receive throughout his American tour frequently seemed to him more intrusive than gratifying.

Boston was then the unchallenged cultural capital of America. Leading American writers together with professors from Harvard University were paraded before Dickens. Washington Irving, whose particular blend of sentimental whimsy and good humour had influenced and delighted Dickens, became an immediate friend. So did Henry Wadsworth Longfellow, whose physical appearance—slim figure, long brown hair, piercing eyes in an alert face—resembled that of the English novelist himself. Charles Dana, author of *Two Years Before the Mast*, was less immediately impressed: dignified Bostonians sometimes saw in Dickens an overdressed little coxcomb. Some hostesses found him illbred; it was whispered that he combed his hair at a dinner table; and prissy gentility was offended when, in discussion of two ladies' relative beauty, Dickens declared, 'Mrs Norton perhaps is the most beautiful but the duchess, to my mind, is the more kissable person.'

The public institutions of Boston impressed Dickens favourably. The Perkins Institute for the

Blind was far in advance of similar English institutions; the South Boston House of Industry was a workhouse which treated paupers with humanity; asylums and prisons were also visited, and in the manufacturing suburb of Lowell, Dickens was delighted to discover that factory girls were given good accommodation, good wages, facilities for saving, and–luxury of luxuries–pianos and circulating libraries. All this seemed to Dickens no excessive recompense for a twelve-hour working day.

From Boston Dickens travelled through New York and Philadelphia to Washington D.C. He visited institutions assiduously on his way south but found little to admire in the prisons of New York and Philadelphia. His reception was also turning a little sour; in a public address, he had mentioned the absence of any international copyright agreement between Britain and America, a state of affairs which led to piracy on both sides of the Atlantic, but by which British writers were the main losers. A howl of newspaper protest at his venturing to criticise his host country stiffened his determination to speak out for those American and British writers he knew to agree with him. His international copyright campaign made him enemies in America, and in spite of the powerful support of Horace Greeley's New York *Tribune* he came to feel himself the victim of universal and hysterical newspaper attack.

In Washington Dickens observed with horror a senate as unprincipled as Westminster's parliament, and markedly more uncouth, baiting John Quincy Adams in his anti-slavery campaign. No politician, it never occurred to him that such an exhibition of boorishness was exactly what the dignified ex-president hoped to elicit from his opponents. Washington Irving was there to be congratulated on his appointment as ambassador to Spain, and President Tyler, now remembered for little but his rhythmical election campaign slogan, 'Tippecanoe and Tyler too', gave Dickens an audience, and expressed his astonishment in finding the great writer to be so young a man. Dickens for his part was astonished that even the president used the spittoon which he found to be disgustingly universal south of New England.

From Washington he went to Richmond, Virginia. Here for the first time he was surrounded by slavery. Dickens hated it. He felt polluted by accepting the service of chattel slaves, and the hospitality of those who bought and sold them. Too many Englishmen– Thackeray was an example–lost their abolitionist principles when they found that slave owners could be hospitable, and uneducated slaves lacked sophisticated manners and charm. To his credit, Dickens was never tempted to flirt with slavery, and with unusual percipience he noted the crude racialism which underlay specious moral and economic arguments. To a southerner who asked if he believed in the Bible, ' "Yes," I said, "but if any man could prove to me that it sanctions slavery, I would place no further credence on it." "Well, then," he said. "By God, sir, the niggers must be kept down, and the whites have put down the coloured people wherever they have found them." "That's the whole question," said I." '

The Dickenses then crossed the Alleghennies, stopping to look at Indian treaties in Harrisburg, and experienced the discomfort and confinement of an airless canal boat to Pittsburg. A steamboat from Pittsburg to Cincinnati and on to Louisville and St Louis was a little more convenient. To a fellow traveller, Dickens looked like a Mississippi river gambler, with his velvet waistcoat and gold pins and chains. To Dickens, his fellow passengers seemed uncouth, ignorant, opinionated, and barbaric. A Choctaw Indian chief impressed him more favourably than any white man he met. This was, after all, frontier territory; but Dickens made no allowance for the hardships and difficulties confronting pioneers. He and Kate suffered from bed bugs in the hotels, and from a public attention which veered from unconcealed, pushful curiosity to uneducated indifference. Democracy was proving to have drawbacks.

North through Ohio the Dickenses travelled to Lake Erie and then to Niagara. The previous year a visit to Glencoe had impressed them hugely–especially as a torrential downpour almost overturned their carriage. But now the grandeur of the Falls supplanted Glencoe in Dickens' mind as the pinnacle of natural majesty. From Niagara they proceeded through Canada, where a visit to a Shaker community left an unfavourable impression of a religion at once joyless and superstitious on Dickens' mind. Their last stop was at Montreal, where a fellow passenger from the *Britannia*, the earl of Mulgrave, was a senior officer at the garrison. At his invitation Dickens organised amateur theatricals for charity. He acted well himself, and, 'Only think', he wrote to Forster, 'of Kate playing! and playing devilish well, I assure you!' Then home to England and the writing of his *American Notes*.

Slave auctions, indoor and out. The really intolerable
evil of America in 1842.

Left :
Henry Wadsworth Longfellow.

Below :
A riverboat on the Mississippi.

Years Abroad

Soon after their return from America the Dickenses were looking forward to a visit from Longfellow who was travelling in Europe. He came and was introduced by them to London society, and was taken on expeditions to the Leather Bottle at Cobham and the Bull at Rochester, scenes of Dickens' boyhood. At Rochester Dickens, Forster and Longfellow disregarded the prohibition on visiting the ancient castle, and scrambling over the barriers clambered all over the tumbling ruin. Longfellow's departure for home, taking with him a copy of the *American Notes*, left Dickens feeling a little flat, and almost immediately he persuaded Maclise, Stanfield and Forster to go on holiday with him to Cornwall.

Dickens proposed a new novel which should open in a remote Cornish village; this seems to have been little more than an excuse for the holiday. The party visited Tintagel, St Michael's Mount and Land's End. Maclise sketched a comic scene: the grave Forster perched on top of the Logan Stone while the others hilariously rocked it. And it was Forster again who sat on the cradle turret of the castle on St Michael's Mount. Maclise himself sketched the romantic St Knighton's waterfall near Tintagel, and exhibited a finished painting later that year of Kate's fifteen-year-old sister Georgina as *The Girl at the Waterfall*—a picture Dickens secretly bought through an agent to prevent the artist making him a present of it.

His next novel, *Martin Chuzzlewit*, opened at a village in Wiltshire rather than Cornwall. Although it was by far the best thing Dickens had written yet, and he knew it, sales were slow. So Dickens took advantage of the serial method of publication and the reading public's presumed interest in his American visit to alter the plot suddenly, and send his hero to America. He was less restrained in his criticism of frontier life than he had been in the American notes, and in Thomas Carlyle's words the book set 'all Yankee-Doodle-dum ablaze like one universal soda bottle'.

The flagging sales produced one of Dickens' characteristic breaks with his publishers. William Hall incautiously commented on the possible loss which might ensue, and Dickens, in a rage, made arrangements for Bradbury and Evans to publish his novels in the future.

But this touchiness was only one sign of a general dissatisfaction with life in England, and the rising expenses of his expanding household. The enormous success of his first special Christmas volume, *A Christmas Carol*, was not enough to prevent him from making arrangements to spend the next year in Italy, where living was cheaper than London. Devonshire Terrace was let, and Dickens set out for the continent with a caravan he described as:

'1 The inimitable Boz.
2 The other half ditto.
3 The sister of ditto ditto.
4 Four babies ranging from two years and a half to seven and a half.
5 Three women servants, commanded by Anne of Broadstairs.'

The party was guided by an invaluable courier, who directed them through Boulogne, Paris, Lyons, Avignon, Marseilles and thence by sea to Genoa. Dickens was always able to win absolutely devoted service from his underlings: Roche the courier, like the temporary secretary who had conducted the Dickenses through the wilder parts of America,

Right:
A visit to the St Gotthard Pass and the Devil's Bridge proved more worthwhile than the St Bernard.

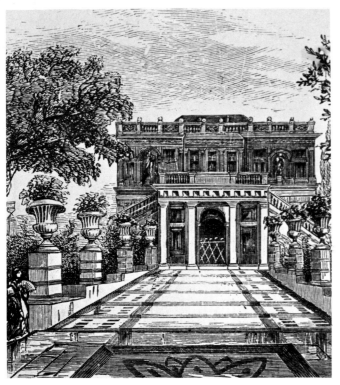

In December he made a flying visit to London to read *The Chimes* to a small audience assembled at Forster's lodgings in Lincoln's Inn Fields. Carlyle attended gravely; Maclise quietly sketched the scene; but the emotional Macready undisguisedly sobbed and cried on the sofa. On his way back to Italy, Dickens stopped in Paris to watch Macready rehearse *Othello*. Then, with the knowledge that his new book was a success, he hurried back to spend Christmas in Genoa.

Here the Dickenses caused a minor sensation; a rich friend had sent an elaborate Twelfth Night cake with extravagant icing sugar ornaments for Charley. A local confectioner, who repaired a corner which had been damaged in transit, displayed the cake in his window, and the Genoese had never seen anything like it.

After Christmas, Dickens and Kate went to Rome to see the carnival and from there travelled down to Naples, which proved disappointing, and made a general tour of Italy on their way back to Genoa. In June the family left Italy, crossing the St Gotthard Pass into Switzerland, where Dickens revelled in the return to a Protestant country. For the rest of 1845 he was back in England, deeply involved in the founding of the *Daily News*, but 1846 found him abroad for another year.

This time Dickens and Kate with Georgina, six children, three servants and the dog Timber Doodle, made their way through Ostend, Worms and Basle to Geneva. Here Dickens began work on *Dombey and Son*, and received distinguished English visitors: Harrison Ainsworth, Tennyson, Nassau Senior, the economist, and Isambard Kingdom Brunel, the engineer among them. A trip to the St Bernard Pass was another disappointment, and *The Battle of Life*, the Christmas book written in Geneva, was perhaps the feeblest piece of writing of Dickens' entire career. But *Dombey*, an examination of family pride and heartlessness in the world of commerce, was a triumph. Although a move from Geneva to Paris demanded much of Dickens' attention, the death of little Paul won back any readers who had been disappointed by his recent work. 'There's no writing against such power as this', exclaimed Thackeray, whose serious reputation was now establishing itself as *Vanity Fair* appeared serially, 'One has no chance!'

In 1847 Charley started school at Eton, and Dickens returned to London. The experiment of living abroad had given him material he was to use in later books, and had temporarily reassured him of financial security. He felt himself a seasoned and cosmopolitan traveller, and saw no need to live overseas again.

Above:
Palazzo Peschiere, the house the Dickens family took in Genoa.

Right:
A picture which echoes the sentiments of The Chimes, *in its warning that the needy should be remembered at Christmas. Nineteenth-century print.*

worked as selflessly on his master's behalf as later employees whose whole careers depended on 'the Chief' were to do.

The Villa di Bella Vista at Albano had been rented for the Dickenses; it turned out to be an enormous pink stucco house with about as much comfort and friendliness as a gaol. Untended gardens and decaying furniture added to the local discomforts of heat, fleas, flies, frogs, stray cats, rats, lizards, scorpions, and the threat of beetles. In Dickens' Protestant eyes these evils were hardly worse than the hordes of priests, monks and Jesuits which offended him everywhere in Italy. At Avignon the Palace of the Popes had shocked him with its memories of the Inquisition. In Italy he loathed the combination of peasant poverty and ecclesiastical splendour. There were a few rewards: in particular, he loved the marionette theatre in Genoa. A death of Napoleon was made especially delightful by a puppet governor of St Helena who ended all his speeches with the word 'Yas!'–an obviously English characteristic!

Before winter the family left the Villa di Bella Vista and moved to the far more comfortable Pallazzo Peschiere, the Palace of the Fishpond. In this magnificent and famous building Dickens began his next Christmas book. ' "We have heard THE CHIMES at midnight, Master Shallow" ', he wrote cryptically to Forster. *The Chimes* was inspired by the government blue books on the conditions of the poor which Dickens had read before leaving England, and was his first explicit attack on the political and economic theorists whose lack of human understanding permitted such conditions.

I WISH YOU ALL A MERRY CHRISTMAS,

AND A HAPPY NEW YEAR.

Animal Magnetism

Doctor John Elliotson, Professor of Medicine at London University, took an interest in the curious fringe areas of his subject. Phrenology, that strange pseudo-science which purported to analyse character from the shape of the head, was encouraged by him, and he became first president of the Phrenological Society. He was also an enthusiastic experimenter with the use of mesmerism to relieve pain. Anton Mesmer had published his discovery of 'animal magnetism' in 1775: he had stumbled across the phenomenon of hypnotism, and his discovery was to be exploited by quacks and charlatans for some time. Elliotson was a respectable physician, but his practice of exhibiting sensational feats performed by hypnotic subjects was injudicious, and led to his resignation from London University. Dickens watched some of his demonstrations with a Belgian boy and two Irish girls, and was introduced by him to the Rev Chauncey Hare Townshend, the author of *Facts in Mesmerism*.

It was in America that Kate lightheartedly offered herself as a subject for mesmeric experiments when Dickens was discussing the topic. Within six minutes Dickens discovered that he could hypnotise: 'I magnetized her into hysterics, and then into magnetic sleep. I tried again next night, and she fell into the slumber in little more than two minutes.' Thereafter he used his power to relieve the intense nervous headaches from which Kate suffered; Georgina, too, became an occasional subject.

But it was in Italy that Dickens' hypnotic skills found their severest test. Emile De la Rue, a Swiss banker, became friendly with the Dickenses in Genoa. His English wife, 'a most affectionate and excellent little woman', suffered from a nervous tic and hallucinations. Dickens suggested to her husband that his magnetic powers might relieve these disabilities,

and with Monsieur De la Rue's consent embarked on a course of treatment. Putting Madame De la Rue into a hypnotic trance, he would encourage her to describe the hallucinatory phantoms which troubled her, and hoped by suggestion to free her of their influence. The treatment proved so successful that Madame De la Rue could not bear to conclude it, and when Charles and Kate travelled from Naples to Rome, they found the De la Rues waiting for them in their hotel. Here the treatment continued: Madame De la Rue's hysterical seizures tended to take place around mid-night, and Kate was disturbed by Charles' prolonged absences in the lady's bedroom, on returning from which he would himself be so emotionally overwrought that he would pace up and down his own room in the small hours of the morning. He described the most severe of these attacks: Monsieur De la Rue took him to his wife's bedroom where

> She was rolled into an apparently impossible ball by tic in the brain and I only knew where her head was by following her long hair to its source. Such a fit had always held her before at least 30 hours and it was so alarming to see that I had hardly any belief in myself in reference to it. But in half an hour she was peacefully and naturally asleep, and next morning the spectres had departed.

Dickens' valuable therapy was becoming indispensable to the lady. An attempt to teach Monsieur De la Rue to hypnotise his own wife failed utterly, and the De la Rues accompanied the Dickenses on their further travels across Italy. Kate, by now, was jealously alarmed. Charles was spending long hours and sharing intense and intimate experiences with the banker's little wife. By the time the party reached Genoa she was no longer speaking to Madame De la Rue, and Dickens, after having made confused apologies for her, found it necessary to explain the truth of her conduct to Emile. Fortunately the banker had complete confidence in his wife and her friend, but Charles was annoyed and humiliated at being suspected, and ten years later, when he had long given up acting as Madame De la Rue's 'animal magnetist', Monsieur De la Rue was still the obvious correspondent to whom he could complain of Kate's 'excruciating jealousy'. She had obtained, he said 'positive proof of my being on the most intimate terms with at least 15,000 women of various conditions in life since we left Genoa. Please to respect me for this vast experience'.

The last view we have of the treatment of Madame De la Rue is of Kate sitting angrily in a coach watching Charles, as with earnest intensity he silently tried to magnetise his patient from a distance.

John Leech, the artist and illustrator of the *Christmas Carol*, was another recipient of Dickens' hypnotic healing. On holiday at Bonchurch on the Isle of Wight, he was mildly concussed while bathing by a blow from a great wave. Ice packs on the head failed to ease the sleep-preventing pain, and although his fretful restlessness made hypnotism difficult, he had succumbed to Dickens' powers within an hour and a half. 'What do you think of my setting up in the magnetic line, with a large brass plate?' asked Dickens. 'Terms, twenty-five guineas per nap.'

It has been suspected that the literally hypnotic power he possessed may have contributed to Dickens' success towards the end of his life in swaying the huge audiences who came to hear him give public readings from his works. This seems unlikely, as he evidently used his talent for acting to 'create' characters in his readings, and must have had his attention on his scripts rather than his audiences. What can be seen is that in his uncompleted novel, *Edwin Drood*, he was giving the villain a hypnotic hold over the heroine. It was characteristic of Dickens to identify himself in some ways with his villains; (he had amazed his friends by remarking that he had put much of himself into Quilp, the sinister, sadistic dwarf of *The Old Curiosity Shop*); the dark side of his personality was something he both recognised and feared, and it is not surprising that although he never abused his mysterious magnetic power, it was so inexplicable as to seem to him a little alarming. Scientific mysteries, like the mythical 'spontaneous combustion' of corrupt bodies which he employed in *Bleak House*, were most safely associated with disreputable characters. Dickens would fully have approved of Du Maurier's Svengali, whose hypnotic power over the young singer Trilby seems implicitly sexual in origin, as is Jasper's over Rosa Bud in *Edwin Drood* and as Dickens may have sensed his own power over Madame De la Rue, not to mention Kate and Georgina, to have been.

Right:
Hypnosis, eighteenth-century print. Dickens was familiar with Mesmer's theories.

Conducted by Charles Dickens

passed over, then another day. I was more wretched. Suddenly I was summoned to the Council Chamber, and an address of peculiar solemnity was made to me. I was told it was high time to turn over a new leaf, and think of becoming a man, if ~~feel~~ I was to do so at all. That it was useless giving me indulgences, as it only had the effect of making me more dissipated and hopelessly abandoned to pleasure; and it was certain if I received any favour or relaxation I would make a bad use of it ~~still~~. Now, would it be any use giving me one more chance? If I was allowed to go out, would I make an exertion for once, and try and learn, and not disgrace us all? &c.; and here the gallows was once more introduced.

In short, it came to this: The Burkenshaws were giving at Tritonville a ball, ~~in fact,~~ and in the kindest manner had asked me. It ~~seemed~~ ~~to be~~ hinted that it was more than probable, ~~should I be brought,~~ my tendency to larceny burglary or other crimes would bring disgrace on the family and interrupt the ball; but still that risk would be run. Provided I showed extra diligence between this time and that, I might be allowed to go.

Now will be understood the significance of the unwonted interest in the vast tailoring preparations ~~which had been set~~ on foot, the gorgeousness of the blue and silver, the velvet collar, and other superb decorations. The costume was pushed on with ardour. A sort of private rehearsal was held the night before, and I was encouraged with the ~~result~~ "that I now looked something like a gentleman, and that if I could only contrive to behave in a cor-

Dickens was a natural journalist. He enjoyed addressing his public directly on the subjects which most concerned him at the moment, and had the good feature writer's confidence that what interested him would interest his readers when marked with his style and personality. *Master Humphrey's Clock* had been one attempt to use the format of the regular miscellaneous journal; it had failed, because the public did not expect such a venture from Dickens at that time. But by the middle of the eighteen-forties, particularly after the shock of *Chuzzlewit's* slipping sales, Dickens was suffering from the creative writer's fear that his imaginative talent might be drying up and with it would go his income. The steady publication of a journal which could at the same time exploit the popularity of his name and also drawn on the talents of other contributors seemed a way of assuring financial security without running the risk of writing himself out. He sounded out Forster on the idea of a weekly magazine, 'price three halfpence, if possible; partly original, partly select; notices of books, notices of theatres, notices of all good things, notices of all bad ones; Carol philosophy [i.e. the generous message of goodwill he had delivered in *A Christmas Carol*], cheerful views, sharp anatomization of humbug, jolly good temper'. This would be called

THE CRICKET

"A Cheerful creature that chirrups on the Hearth"
Natural History.

Forster, himself an experienced journalist, dismissed this idea, and it only survived in *The Cricket on the Hearth*, the Christmas book for 1845. Consideration of the market led Dickens to a new idea; a daily newspaper with a liberal outlook to rival the Whig *Morning Chronicle* and the powerful *Times*. Bradbury and Evans agreed to put up some capital for such a ven-

ture and to be its publishers. Joseph Paxton agreed to become another leading backer: he had made his fortune in railway speculation before he made his lasting name as designer of the Crystal Palace, and he saw to it that the paper should give full coverage to the vast railway expansions and share transactions of the eighteen-forties. Two north country liberal capitalists supplied further backing, and Dickens appointed himself editor at a salary of £2000 a year.

Now began the work of assembling the newspaper's staff. Experienced journalists were attracted from the *Morning Chronicle* and the *Economist*. William Henry Wills, the assistant editor of *Chambers Journal*, who had contributed to *Bentley's Miscellany* and *Punch* in previous years, became Dicken's personal secretary and general administrative assistant. He was so thin that Douglas Jerrold wondered whether he ever tried to crawl down a gas-pipe or shut himself up in a flute-case. But with utter reliability and a lack of any distracting imagination he was to be Dickens' loyal and trusted right-hand man in all subsequent journalistic ventures. Forster disliked Wills, but Dickens knew that he could not have found a better second-in-command. The *Daily News* found employment for Dickens' father and father-in-law; George Hogarth became its music critic, and John Dickens, in his last employment, was head of the reporting staff. He organised the efficient delivery of news from parliament to Fleet Street, and as he was not called upon to write it himself, his rotund Micawberish style was no drawback. Almost daily his pocket-handkerchief was stolen as he walked down the Strand to the *Daily News* office, for he had not the time to give chase to pickpockets if the parliamentary reports were to meet the newspaper's deadlines, and anyway, he was by now too fat and slow to have any hope of catching up

Left:
Galley proof with corrections in Dickens' hand.

Above:
Broadstairs, Dickens' favourite resort.

Right:
The interior of Dickens' Broadstairs house.

with them. Among the reporters working under his direction were sons of Douglas Jerrold and William Hazlitt.

The eccentric Richard Hengist Horne was also on the staff. Horne was a 'spasmodic' poet who had published his epic *Orion* at the retail price of one farthing, provided the would-be purchaser could pronounce its title correctly. He submitted pieces of journalism to Dickens for several years, until his general lack of success led him to emigrate to Australia. Here he had a surprising turn of fortune (like Mr Micawber), proving a daring and resourceful bush law-enforcer, according to the reminiscences he published. Alas, these were only loosely based on fact: Horne had actually proved as inadequate in the outback as one might expect of a sensitive, unathletic, literary man. And shortly before Dickens died he was back in England, looking to old friends to support him.

Punch friends helped with sub-editing: Jerrold and Lemon worked with able Fleet Street men. And the team of leader writers was outstanding: William Jonson Fox, the most persuasive advocate of removing the protective tax from wheat in order that the poor might have cheap bread, headed the team. As a Unitarian minister he lent respectability, in addition to his journalistic talent, to any venture with which he was associated. Forster and Albany Fonblanque also contributed, and on Wednesday, 21 January 1846, Dickens outlined the paper's principles in its first

TITANIA DICKENS TO BOTTOM, THE DAILY NEWS.

Come rest in this bosom, my own stricken donkey,
Nor heed *Times*, nor *Chronicle*, *Grandm'a*, nor *Flunkey*;
Though the leaders are scorned of my own *Daily News*,
I who wrote them, to read them will never refuse.

What's an editor made for, if he isn't the brick,
Circulation or none, to his paper to stick?

I know not, I ask not, if they buy you or not,
I but know that I edit thee—therefore they ought.

Thou hast called me thy " Dickens " in moments of bliss,
Still *the* Dickens I'll play with thee even in this;
While there's shot in the locker thy fortune is mine,
While a copper is left I am *thy* Valentine!

published number–'Principles of Progress and Improvement, of Education, Civil and Religious Liberty, Equal Legislation.'

Before twenty numbers had appeared, Dickens left the editor's chair. It had not occurred to him that as editor he might not be dictator of the paper's policy. When he found that the paper's owners–particularly Bradbury–interfered in its running, he withdrew his guiding hand, leaving Forster to take over. It was probably a wise decision. He had given the paper his enthusiasm and energy, without which it might never have started, but he was now a writer rather than a routine journalist. In spite of the great names he had assembled, the paper had not shaken its rivals as they had feared it would. Nor did it ever come to rival the massive circulation of the *Times*. Less dynamic figures would be needed to carry it through the difficult opening years of its establishment, although even after the *Daily News* had amalgamated with the *Morning Chronicle* to become the *News Chronicle*, the association with Dickens as first editor remained a proud memory.

Experience was never wasted on Dickens. He learnt from the *Daily News* venture that it was impossible for him to work for an independent management. When he again turned his mind to producing a journal he recognised that he must be its controlling owner. He had suggested to Forster in 1849 a sort of weekly gossip sheet in which a 'SHADOW' would fall across various places, political scandals, and humbugs in London. He hoped that the *Shadow*'s opinions would be something the public would come to anticipate eagerly. Forster was as unsympathetic to this notion as he had been to *The Cricket*. But this time Dickens was determined to have his private miscellany, and in 1850 he hurled possible titles at Forster: *The Microscope, The Holly Tree, The Rolling Years, The Comrade, Charles Dickens : A weekly journal designed for the instruction and entertainment of all classes of readers : Conducted by Himself, The Household Voice, The Household Face*. And at last *Household Words* was accepted, with the Shakespearian epigraph 'Familiar in their mouths as Household Words'. The domestic bias of the titles was no accident; the market was now ready for just such a respectable middle-brow magazine as Dickens proposed. The cheap magazines of the eighteen-forties had become increasingly sensational and pornographic in tone. Reaction was now setting in, and Dickens was meeting a real need of that Victorian bourgeoisie whose tastes and attitudes he shared to so great an extent–a need for undemanding reading material which should be morally inoffensive.

Wills was brought in as sub-editor at a salary of eight pounds a week and an eighth share in the profits; Horne contributed articles for a short time, and a group of unknowns often referred to as 'Dickens' young men' made regular contributions : G. A. Sala, whose mother had known Dickens a decade earlier, Edmond Yates, Percy Fitzgerald, and, closest to Dickens, Wilkie Collins. Occasional contributors made

THE MISTLETOE BOUGH; or, CHRISTMAS FESTIVITIES.

A popular view of Christmas, which Dickens picked up and intensified in his Christmas books. From the Gallery of Comicalities, *1838.*

Left, above :
The slow start of the Daily News *after the proud claims made for it was a relief to Fleet Street. Professional journalists laughed at novelist Dickens acting as editor. And this cartoonist has not overlooked the connection with* Punch. *From a woodcut illustration in* Mephistopheles, *1846.*

Left, below :
Dickens reading The Chimes *to friends in Forster's rooms in Lincolns Inn Fields.*

Chair Proprietor. "WOULD YOU PLEASE TO PAY FOR THE CHEERS, MUM?"
Lady. "HOW MUCH?"
Chair Proprietor. "WELL, MUM—HOW MANY MIGHT YOU BE A SITTIN' ON?"

up a striking list of distinguished Victorian writers: Mrs Gaskell, Bulwer Lytton, Charles Reade, Mrs Craik, Sheridan Le Fanu, Coventry Patmore and Harriet Martineau. Although he greatly admired her first novel, and correctly surmised that the pseudonym George Eliot concealed a woman's hand, Dickens was unable to persuade Marian Evans (or Lewes) to let him have *Adam Bede* for *Household Words*.

Copies of the little journal look very dreary to twentieth-century eyes. Double columns of small print, unbroken by any illustration, hardly strike us as ideal popular entertainment. But the formula Dickens devised was entirely successful in its time. Serialised novels and short stories gave the relief of fiction; instructive articles on subjects ranging from the use of machinery in farming to the tracing of coal from primeval forest to factory furnace satisfied the Victorian craving for information; books old and new were discussed and anecdotes about their authors mingled with biographical sketches of other historical personages; and, in each number, two or at most three articles would take up the great social concerns dear to Dickens. Readers of *Household Words* would become familiar with the idea that education and improved social conditions were a better answer to crime than elaborate prison buildings. They would be shown how slums were not only evil in themselves, but breeding grounds of disease and moral squalor by which the East End could infect the West End. The complacency of civic dignitaries, the self-satisfaction of members of the establishment, and the inefficiencies of conventional administration were all targets which *Household Words* scored off. And yet all this serious content was contained in the liveliest language Dickens could wring from his contributors or compose

A cartoon drawn for Punch *by Dickens' friend John Leech.*

Right:
Past and Present: *a dramatic picture by Augustus Egg, Dickens' friend, of the 'every picture tells a story' kind that the Victorians loved. This scene of discovered adultery has the kind of drama Dickens himself used in his novels.*

himself. 'Brighten it, brighten it, brighten it', he ordered Wills. No mere compilation of statistics would sell: Faraday's scientific lectures could be offered back to readers through the imagined words of a small boy who had heard and understood them; parody of the *Arabian Nights* made a splendid vehicle for political satire; imagination was hailed wherever it was encountered by Dickens, and encouraged in writers for his journal.

Control was firmly in Dickens' hands. He owned half the paper; one eighth of the profits went to Wills, another eighth was owned by Forster, and Bradbury and Evans were left with a quarter of the total as their share. Since Wills was entirely dependent on Dickens and Forster was an unshakeably loyal ally, Dickens had effectively three-quarters control. This meant that throughout the journal's life he could be—and was—ruthlessly dictatorial on matters of content and style. Contributors who had not conformed had their work re-written if they contradicted Dickens known views. All articles were unsigned, but Dickens' name was firmly printed across the front page, an arrangement which had led such friends as Douglas Jerrold to refuse their assistance—not anonymous but 'mononymous', Jerrold had called the arrangement. Dickens' absolute power was revealed conclusively when he

determined to close the journal down against the wishes of the publishers.

The break with Bradbury and Evans came after 1857, when Dickens had very injudiciously composed a public statement concerning his domestic difficulties which he printed in *Household Words*. He also sent this confession of marital disharmony to other journals with the request that they print it; some did, but some, like *Punch*, refused to do so, both out of consideration for Dickens and Kate, and because it would be inappropriate material for such a periodical. Dickens was behaving quite unreasonably under the stress of his unhappiness, and was particularly incensed that *Punch*, edited by his old friend Lemon, and printed by his own publishers, should refuse his statement. In pique, he returned to Chapman and Hall as publishers of his novels, and demanded that Bradbury and Evans also dissociate themselves from *Household Words*. They refused, in spite of the threat conveyed by Forster that Dickens would remove himself from the 'conductor's' chair, advertise the fact that he was doing so, and start a rival journal. Hopefully they brought a suit against Dickens to prevent him from injuring their joint property. The courts recognised that Dickens could not be compelled to edit a journal of which he was the controlling shareholder, and ordered that *Household Words* should be auctioned. Bradbury and Evans were bought out for three and a half thousand pounds at the auction, and Dickens' new journal *All the Year Round* was able to add 'with which is incorporated *Household Words*' to its title.

The title had caused a little difficulty; Forster had been horrified that Dickens, in the throes of a highly publicised marital breakdown, should propose calling his new periodical *Household Harmony*. Ownership involved less argument; Dickens took three quarters of the venture and Wills the remaining quarter. The old policy of anonymity was altered in as much as the authors of the serialised novels which now occupied the front page were acknowledged–Dickens' *Tale of Two Cities* set the ball rolling here. With three quarters of the profits coming directly to him he was able to reduce his own editor's salary from the £5000 a year he had taken from *Household Words* to £500 a year. Sale of the right to publish an American edition immediately after publication of each number in England brought Dickens another £1000 a year. Otherwise, all policy was unchanged in the transfer from one magazine to the other.

According to Lord Northcliffe, Dickens was the greatest magazine editor of his own or any other age. This is probably true from the point of view of popular, commercial journalism. Dickens made less important literary discoveries than such editors as Frank Harris and Ford Madox Ford; the journalism he supervised has not itself remained a living part of our literature as has that of the eighteenth-century journalists he admired and hoped to imitate–Addison and Goldsmith. But he reached, entertained, and influenced a vast and important audience in his own time. *All the Year Round* reached the amazing circulation of 300,000. (*Household Words* had hit 40,000–the level of sales which had seemed astonishing in *Pickwick*). And from the time *Household Words* was founded to the end of his life, Dickens was constantly engaged in writing, supervising and directing a journal which had to appear every week. This astonishing background to the activities and turmoil of his later years is a measure of the extraordinary energy he brought to the whole of his life.

Criminology and Social Work

'Orrible murder', central subject of many a melo-drama, fascinates a wide public without other morbid inclinations, and it fascinated Dickens. Murders give energy to the plots of many of his novels; when there are no actual killings there may be other forms of crime. Dickens' love of the vivid and flamboyant associates easily with an interest in the sensational.

In his earliest days this led him to a predilection for walking through the criminal slums of London–Seven Dials and Saffron Hill especially. The quantities of stolen handkershiefs to be seen publicly displayed for sale in Saffron Hill gave him inspiration for Fagin's gang in *Oliver Twist*. When Longfellow visited England, a trip to the more obnoxious and squalid areas of the metropolis was organised by Dickens as an eye-opener for the elegant Bostonian.

This sight-seeing tour of the waterside thieves' dens was conducted by officers supplied by the governors of two London prisons. Captain G. L. Chesterton, governor of Coldbath Fields House of Correction, and Lieutenant A. F. Tracey, governor of the Westminster Bridewell at Tothill Fields, were friends whose work as reforming governors Dickens greatly admired. Un-reformed prisons–Newgate was a principle example in Dickens' lifetime–exhibited all the faults to be seen in the Newgate of *The Beggar's Opera*: no adequate provision of food or clothing for prisoners without means; bribery and corruption rife amongst the turn-keys, and all prisoners, except those under sentence of death, promiscuously mingled together, so that the first offender might find prison a veritable university of crime. Chesterton and Tracey, both able disciplin-arians, had stamped out corruption amongst their staff, and persuaded the magistrates supervising their prisons to provide adequate food and clothing for prisoners, at the same time as they dropped the system of permitting wealthy prisoners to bring their own creature comforts into the gaol. They were then faced with the problem of the prisoners' idleness and the de-moralisation and vice which resulted from ceaseless confined loafing. When, in 1837, Dickens and a group of friends visited Newgate, Macready observed that a man waiting to be hanged for rape seemed the most cheerful inmate of the prison: 'In all the pride of our nature seemed eradicated or trodden down–it was a most depressing sight.'

Apart from taking obvious steps like separating the male prisoners from the female, Chesterton and Tracey followed the policy of giving them irksome labour and having close watch kept on them to see that they did not talk to each other while working. Infringements of the rule of silence were punished severely with flogging. The prisoners' days were passed in oakum-picking, labour at the treadmill, or the passing of heavy lead shots from hand to hand in the yard. Their work was deliberately made useless as they then hated it the more. Severe retribution was the prisons' aim: Chesterton and Tracey were reasonably humane men, but they were coolly realistic, and doubted whether most of their charges could be reformed or re-habilitated.

It was not unusually progressive of Dickens to support these men's prison reforms. The unreformed

Above:
A hulk : old men-of-war, anchored and used as convict-ships, were among the worst types of unreformed prison. Dickens used hulks as a sinister background to Great Expectations. *From an etching by E. W. Cooke, 1828.*

Right:
The exercise yard in unreformed Newgate. From Jerrold and Doré's London.

Melancholy end of CORINTHIAN KATE One of those lamentable examples of dissipated life in London

The squalid end of a low-class prostitute as seen in a coloured print. The great achievement of Dickens and Miss Coutts was to enable girls to escape from conditions like this.

A comment on attempts to clean up the streets of London from Gallery of Comicalities, 1843. *The poor feared that such action would only lead to blackmail and corruption on the part of the police.*

prisons had no serious defenders in the nineteenth century; the only case for them was that it was cheaper to lock men and women up together in large buildings, letting them find their own keep, than to supply constant incorruptible guards and the means of subsistence for convicts. Dickens' most important contribution to the Victorian debate on prison reform was his powerful opposition to the most advanced and idealistic proposal, the so called 'separate system'.

America had already established a long penological lead over Europe. On balance, Dickens thought Chesterton's and Tracey's prisons were better conducted than those he saw in America running on similar principles with prisoners working together in silence. But the jewel of the American prison system was not 'silent' Sing Sing, but 'separate' Cherry Hill, the Philadelphia penitentiary. Dickens toured this, and described it in one of the most memorable chapters in the *American Notes*. The integrity and dedication of the staff was above question. Nonetheless Dickens thought they did not know what they were doing, and the form of imprisonment they administered 'torture and agony', 'prolonged for years'.

Prisoners at Cherry Hill were kept in separate cells and never allowed to see each other. The cells were reasonably furnished with work benches and water closets, and the men spent their days working in solitude. Rare prison visitors, guards bringing meals and the prison chaplain were their sole contacts with humanity. Defenders of the system argued that solitude aided the religious conversion which seemed a necessary pre-requisite of rehabilitation, and pointed out that punishments were rare under the separate system. Opponents argued that encouraging criminals to profess Christianity was tantamount to encouraging humbug, and observed appositely that after huge sums had been spent in erecting prisons where solitary inmates had negligible opportunities to misbehave, it was foolish to boast of the infrequency of punishments. Dickens leapt at once to the most objectionable feature of the system: it was a system of solitary confinement, whatever its defenders might choose to say about prison visits and the attention of the chaplain. As such it imposed an intolerable mental burden on men whose very presence there showed their incapacity to bear it. The more robust prisoners canted hypo-

No. VII. MORALS IN DANGER; OR, MILLINERS CORRECTED.

"Come, my pretty lass, I sees you vants a protector, so jist valk vith me to the station-house; ve takes petikler care o' young vomen there. Don't tell me you'r nothing but a milliner's gal; I knows better—you're a common street valker; and this is not the first time I've seed you on my beat. The Hact must be obeyed, and the morals of the public presarved."

critically of the benefit imprisonment had been to them; long term offenders brought to the doors of their cells seemed to Dickens like wan figures called up from their graves. It was over Dickens' strong opposition that the model 'separate' prison of Pentonville was built in London. The humbugging and mollycoddling aspect of chaplain-dominated solitude are comically well brought out in *David Copperfield* as Uriah Heep and Mr Littimer easily establish, to the satisfaction of visiting magistrates, the moral superiority of their penitence for felony over David's innocence.

' "Before I come here", said Uriah, stealing a look at us, as if he would have blighted the outer world to which we belonged, if he could, "I was given to follies; but now I am sensible of my follies. There's a deal of sin outside. There's a deal of sin in mother. There's nothing but sin everywhere—except here."
"You are quite changed?" said Mr Creakle.
"Oh dear, yes, sir!" cried this hopeful penitent.
"You wouldn't relapse, if you were going out?" asked somebody else.
"Oh de-ar no, sir!"
"Well!" said Mr Creakle, "this is very gratifying. You have addressed Mr Copperfield, Twenty Seven. Do you wish to say anything further to him?"
"You knew me a long time before I came here and was changed, Mr Copperfield," said Uriah, looking at me; and a more villainous look I never saw, even on his visage. "You knew me when, in spite of my follies, I was umble among them that was proud, and meek among them that was violent—you was violent to me yourself, Mr Copperfield. Once, you struck me a blow on the face, you know."
General commiseration. Several indignant glances directed at me.'

When Uriah patronisingly reflects on his mother's sinfulness, he only echoes the actual sentiments of a prisoner in Reading gaol, boastfully quoted by its fatuous chaplain in his defence of the separate system. Pentonville, and the unhealthily sited 'separate' Millbank, suffered epidemics of sickness, neurosis and mental breakdown, and outbursts of suicide unknown under the more rigorous silent system. Dickens was the most influential opponent of separation, and we should remember that to his credit, even while we bear in mind that his ruthlessly punitive attitude to adult male offenders led him to favour the extensive use of the treadmill and the whip.

His severity did not extend to endorsing the gallows. He saw three public executions in his lifetime: two hangings in England and a beheading in Italy. (He may also have seen a Swiss headsman). On each occasion he was revolted and wrote powerfully in protest. *Barnaby Rudge* contained explicit objections to the old penal code, and in the character of Dennis the hangman showed both the brutalising effects of public execution on its practitioners and the demoralisation of its victims.

"That I should come to be worked off!" he cries, as he awaits his own execution, "I, I! That *I* should come!" "And why not?" said Hugh, as he thrust back his matted hair to get a better view of his late associate. "How often, before I knew your trade, did I hear you talking of this as if it was a treat?"
"I an't inconsistent", screamed the miserable creature; "I'd talk so again, if I was hangman. Some other man has got my old opinions at this minute. That makes it worse. Somebody's longing to work me off. I know by myself that somebody must be."

This was written in 1841, a year after Dickens had witnessed the public execution of the murderer Courvoisier.

In 1846 he wrote four public letters to the *Daily News* in which he put his view of the case against capital punishment. He was not so much concerned with the sufferings of murderers as with the effects of their execution on society. The whole ritual of hanging, he felt, lent a morbid fascination to what might otherwise be properly regarded as a squalid crime. And might not murderers feel that in risking the justice of 'an eye for an eye' they entitled to themselves to take life? He quoted statistics to prove that capital punishment had no demonstrable effect as a deterrent. In these letters, he presented his case cogently and lucidly in the most sustained piece of argument on a social topic to be found in his writings.

In 1849 Dickens went with John Leech to witness the public execution of Mr and Mrs Manning, a sordid pair who had murdered their lodger in Bermondsey and buried him under the kitchen floor. Mrs Manning was a passionate Belgian, whom Dickens used as the model for Hortense, the murderess in *Bleak House*. Leach had been commissioned by *Punch* to illustrate the scene as part of *Punch*'s abolitionist campaign. Dickens wrote two highly influential letters to the *Times* opposing the public spectacle of execution. The levity of the crowd had disgusted him, and he urged that after conviction murderers should be confined from public sight and hanged privately within prison walls. When public execution was abolished in 1868, many people remembered Dickens as one of the great advocates of this change.

Although the convicted felon aroused little but repugnance in Dickens, and he believed that some souls were so evil that nothing short of their perpetual imprisonment could adequately safeguard society, he did not believe that high crime rates were inevitable. Education was the cure he believed in, and he was one of the earliest supporters of the Ragged Schools movement, which tried to bring literacy to the deprived and delinquent children of the slums. In *Our Mutual Friend* Dickens jibed at the squalid buildings, overcrowding, inadequate teachers, and infantile moral instruction of such places. His comic and critical sense took over in the composition of his novel. But in private life he recognised that such schools tackled a difficult, thankless and vital task with appallingly inadequate

A ragged school, c. 1856.

means and conditions. Likewise he supported Mechanics' Institutes for the education of working men, and was a willing speaker on their behalf, although he had laughed at their solemnities in the *Sketches*.

But the most sustained and admirable piece of social work he undertook was the establishment and running of a home for fallen women in Shepherds Bush. Angela Burdett Coutts, heir to two fortunes and distinguished Victorian philanthropist, had made the acquaintance of the Dickenses shortly after Charles' rise to fame. She became a friend and regular correspondent, and remained the only woman whom Dickens treated with respect as an intellectual equal, without romantic idealisation. Dickens frequently advised her on the charitable use of her money, and helped her with the difficult task of distinguishing between fraudulent and truly needy begging-letter writers. In 1846 Miss Coutts was seized with an ambition to do something for the depressed harlots who infested the Victorian streets. She proposed to open a reformatory home for them, and consulted Dickens as to how this might best be done. Dickens responded with enthusiasm, energy, compassion and commonsense. He advised her not to lay too heavy a stress on reform as a matter of penitence and recompense to society; reform was a way by which the girls could find happier lives for themselves, and he and Miss Coutts agreed that emigration to Australia with the prospect of a new life was the conclusion to be aimed at. Where, left to herself, Miss Coutts might have overplayed moralising, preaching and religion in the running of the homes, Dickens stressed the acquisition of the useful household skills, and encouraged the practice of such harmless recreations as music and gardening. He personally supervised the finding and furnishing of a suitable house in Acton Road, Shepherds Bush, wrote a rather gushy public letter of invitation to prostitutes to enter it, saw to the appointment of suitable matrons, and with the help of Chesterton selected the first inmates.

He trod an admirable line between idealism and cynicism. Where Miss Coutts assumed that voluntary celibacy would be accepted for life by redeemed whores, Dickens tactfully pointed out that the aspiration of marriage in the colonies would be a reasonable goal for them to set themselves, and should not be opposed. On the other hand, when Chesterton assumed that known drunkards would have to be refused admission to the home, Dickens disagreed. Although the middle-aged alcoholic would, he thought, be past the power of the home to help, hard liquor was an inevitable adjunct of a life of criminal vice, and if young women could be weaned from the one then they should be able to give up the other. The home was as far removed as possible from a penitentiary in appearance—the bedrooms were so neatly and cleanly furnished that one deprived girl burst into tears on seeing this evidence of a new life—but cautious rules and careful supervision were not to be

overlooked. The matrons were ordered to keep linen cupboards locked so that girls whose past acquaintance inevitably included criminal receivers should not be subjected to undue temptation to theft, and Dickens saw to it that hard cases whose intention of reform was nonexistent were expelled from the home if they passed his scrutiny of applicants and gained admission. But their life was deliberately not made cloistered and free from temptation; the aim was that they should ultimately stand on their own feet, and so they had to be allowed to go out of the home and about their business while they prepared for independence.

A system of good and bad marks for conduct was maintained, and the acquisition of sufficient good marks was rewarded with small cash payments, about equal to the wages of domestic servants. But the system was realistic; although bad marks were given, it was taken for granted that girls would from time to time swear, malinger, and behave obstreperously. Most admirably realistic of all, Dickens held out no hopes of a high rate of success in reforming the girls. About 50 per cent passing through to new and useful lives in the colonies seemed to him a reasonable target. This was an accurate prognostication of the success rate; in the first six years of its existence, Urania Cottage, as the house was called, saw twenty-nine out of a total of fifty-six inmates acquire good characters in Australia. Of the remainder, seven discharged themselves during the probationary period Dickens had insisted all women should undergo on admission; ten were expelled, and seven ran away without warning. Another three fell back into evil ways on the passage out to Australia.

For nearly ten years after 1846 Dickens was closely involved with the working of Urania Cottage. He visited it regularly, lectured and dismissed recalcitrant girls as the need arose, investigated doubtful reports of misconduct, and sent Miss Coutts frequent accounts of the use to which her money was being put. The whole conduct of the venture was marked with the personal touch of his humanity. He rejected uniforms of a strong, sound, cheap material on the grounds that it lacked colour, and colour was vital in the lives of women accustomed to crude sensation. He could be amused as well as indignant at the impertinence of some of the failures—of Little Willis, for example, who objected to losing good conduct marks:

"Oh!" she said "I could wish not to have my marks took away."–"Exactly so," said I. "That's quite right; and the only way to get them back again, is to do as well as you can."–"Ho! But if she didn't have 'em give up at once, she could wish fur to go".–"Very well", said I. "You shall go tomorrow morning."

He was alert to the dangers of institutionalisation, noting that girls who in their own squalid surroundings were compassionate to each other in sickness seemed strangely heartless when others undertook the

Above:
Angela Burdett Coutts.
Left, above:
An American convict in his separate cell: clean, occupied, but solitary.
Left, below:
Prostitutes in the Haymarket. From Mayhew's London Labour and the London Poor.

nursing. His cure for this was, of course, to give them more responsibility and the matron less, for their own wellbeing.

Lastly he took a proper pride and delight in the home's successes. In 1856 one Louisa Cooper came back from the Cape and visited the home's committee. Dickens was delighted to see her 'nicely dressed and looking well-to-do', although she brought him a present, 'the most hideous Ostrich's Egg ever laid— wrought all over with frightful devices, the most tasteful of which represents Queen Victoria (with her crown on) standing on top of a Church receiving professions of affection from a British Seaman'. He richly deserved such human rewards for his long, steady and selfless work.

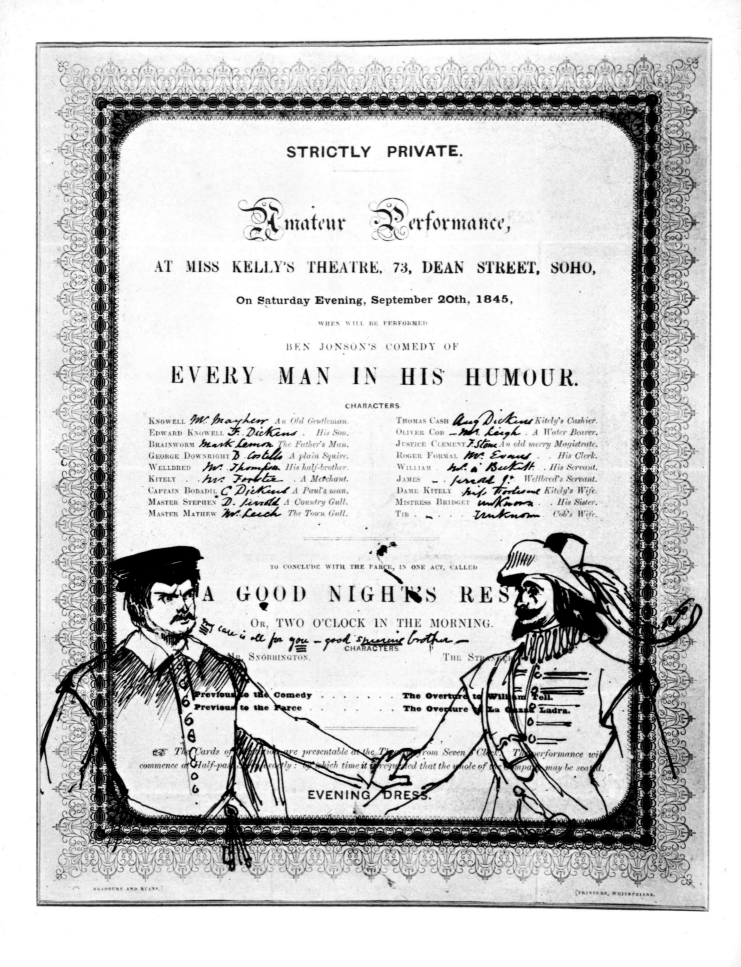

STRICTLY PRIVATE.

Amateur Performance,

AT MISS KELLY'S THEATRE, 73, DEAN STREET, SOHO,

On Saturday Evening, September 20th, 1845,

WHEN WILL BE PERFORMED

BEN JONSON'S COMEDY OF

EVERY MAN IN HIS HUMOUR.

CHARACTERS

KNOWELL *Mr. Mayhew* *An Old Gentleman.*	THOMAS CASH *Aug Dickens* *Kitely's Cashier.*
EDWARD KNOWELL *F. Dickens* *His Son.*	OLIVER COB *Mr. Leigh* *A Water Bearer.*
BRAINWORM *Mark Lemon* *The Father's Man.*	JUSTICE CLEMENT *F. Stone* *An old merry Magistrate.*
GEORGE DOWNRIGHT *D. Costello* *A plain Squire.*	ROGER FORMAL *Mr. Evans* *His Clerk.*
WELLBRED *Mr. Thompson* *His half-brother.*	WILLIAM *W. à Beckett* *His Servant.*
KITELY *Mr. Forster* *A Merchant.*	JAMES *Jerrold Jr* *Wellbred's Servant.*
CAPTAIN BOBADIL *C. Dickens* *A Paul's man.*	DAME KITELY *Miss Woolson* *Kitely's Wife.*
MASTER STEPHEN *D. Jerrold* *A Country Gull.*	MISTRESS BRIDGET *unknown* *His Sister.*
MASTER MATHEW *Mr. Leech* *The Town Gull.*	TIB *unknown* *Cob's Wife.*

TO CONCLUDE WITH THE FARCE, IN ONE ACT, CALLED

A GOOD NIGHT'S RES[T]

OR, TWO O'CLOCK IN THE MORNING.

My care is all for you — good sneezing brother —

CHARACTERS.

MR. SNOBBINGTON. THE STRA[NGER]

Previous to the Comedy	The Overture to William Tell.
Previous to the Farce	The Overture to La Gazza Ladra.

☞ *The Cards of [Admission] are presentable at the [Theatre] from Seven o'Clock. The performance will commence at Half-past [Seven] exactly: by which time it is required that the whole of the company may be seated.*

EVENING DRESS.

BRADBURY AND EVANS.] [PRINTERS, WHITEFRIARS.

Amateur
Theatricals

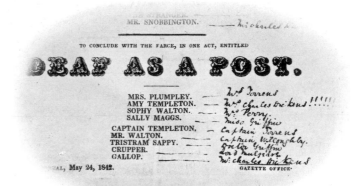

Although there is no definite proof, it seems probable that when he was a clerk Dickens had appeared on the stages of those small private theatres which, in the early nineteenth century, charged a low fee for seats, and a fluctuating scale of fees to members of the general public who wished to take part in the plays performed. He referred amusingly in the *Sketches* to enthusiastic young men enacting Richard the Third who barked, 'Orf with his 'ed!' and then sneered slowly, 'So much for B-u-u-uckingham'.

The first appearance on stage of Dickens as a gentleman amateur was at Montreal in 1842, in the Earl of Musgrave's garrison theatricals. But during the eighteen-forties and 'fifties he must have been the leading amateur actor in England.

On his Christmas visit to London in 1844 to read *The Chimes*, Dickens had suggested to Forster that they might gather together a company of amateurs to perform a play. On his return from Italy the following year work began on a production of Ben Jonson's *Every Man in His Humour*. Frances Kelly, a retired actress, owned a small theatre in Dean Street, Soho, which she leased out to small troupes for rehearsal purposes and to Dickens' company of amateurs. Dickens' friends were pressed into service: Stanfield and Maclise suffered from stage fright and begged off acting, though Stanfield became an invaluable stage manager; Forster and Dickens' brothers Fred and Augustus were recruited; Frank Stone the artist was another performer, and from *Punch* came the editor, Mark Lemon, John Leech and Douglas Jerrold. Dickens energetically cleaned up Miss Kelly's

Playbill for the first performance of the amateur company. Maclise has sketched his friends Forster and Dickens in costume.

theatre, greatly surprising her own small staff—a silent man who was inseparable from his straw hat, and an excitable little girl, whose amazed squeals and giggles at the goings on of the amateurs led them to nickname her 'Fireworks'. The company was worked hard; Dickens and Lemon got down to such menial work as numbering seats in their shirt sleeves; and the well-advertised performance was fully attended by friends of the company. On the night, Dean Street was crowded with carriages, and an extra force of police had to guard the doors of the theatre. Tennyson, the Duke of Devonshire, Lady Holland and the Carlyles were among the distinguished audience. The Carlyles were unimpressed. '*O how expensive!*' commented Jane Carlyle disapprovingly. Her husband sniffed at 'poor little Dickens, all painted in black and red, and affecting the voice of a man of six feet'. But Macready thought that 'several of the actors were very fine as amateurs', and the rest of the audience could find no fault in Dickens as Captain Bobadil.

The fame of the venture was such that the public clamoured for a repeat performance, and it was ultimately decided that the same production might be staged again as a charity benefit for Doctor Southwood Smith's nursing home. The larger St James' theatre was booked for this occasion, and Prince Albert himself headed an audience containing Prince George of Cambridge, the Duke of Wellington, Lord Melbourne, and Baron de Rothschild. Early in 1846 the production was performed again at Miss Kelly's theatre, the profits this time being handed over to her.

Theatricals crept into Dickens' private life at this time; his own resplendent waistcoats seemed too drab for a wedding he had to attend, and he begged the loan of a blue and purple striped stage waistcoat worn by Macready in Bulwer Lytton's play *Money*.

In 1847, the company, augmented by Augustus Egg, George Cruikshank, and G.H.Lewes, the popular scientific journalist who was to be best known as George Eliot's common-law husband, was re-assembled. A series of benefit performances of *Every Man in His Humour* and *The Merry Wives of Windsor* in London and the provinces was proposed, with the object of paying off Leigh Hunt's debts. Before performances began, Hunt was granted a government pension, so the London productions and *The Merry Wives* were dropped from the scheme. But the company enjoyed themselves touring Manchester and Liverpool, and Dickens wrote a fragment of an account of the tour as witnessed by Mrs Gamp. She expressed herself strongly on the subject of Dickens himself in conversation with Mr Wilson, the company's wig maker:

> "Have I not the pleasure," he said, looking at me curious, "of addressing Mrs Gamp?"
> "Gamp I am, sir," I replies. "Both by name and nature."
> "Would you like to see your beeograffer's moustache and whiskers, ma'am?" he says. "I've got 'em in this box."
> "Drat my beeographer, sir," I says, "He has given me no region to wish to know anythink about him."

The carefully curled beared and moustache Dickens wore as Captain Bobadil, and which reappeared, drooping and bedraggled after Bobadil's humiliation, were a notable feature of his make-up.

The following year the twin aims of assisting the playwright Sheridan Knowles and purchasing Shakespeare's house at Stratford for the nation led to the performance of *The Merry Wives of Windsor* at last. *Every Man in His Humour* was alternated with it, and Queen Victoria attended a performance at the Theatre Royal, Haymarket. The company then went on to Manchester, Liverpool and Birmingham, and Dickens seems to have enjoyed himself as much in entertaining them on their long railway journeys, buying huge quantities of buns at station refreshment rooms and seeing to their elaborate receptions, with flowers for the ladies, at the great hotels they almost filled, as he did in playing Shallow to Lemon's Falstaff. Scotland clamoured to be included in this tour, so with Macready's professional manager to attend to the staging in strange theatres the troupe went on to Glasgow and Edinburgh, and took more than £2000 by the end of the tour.

1849 was a year of acting in great country houses. In Lausanne, the Dickenses had met the Honourable Richard and Mrs Watson, and subsequently stayed with them at their invitation in Rockingham Castle,

their beautiful Tudor stately home. Here they enjoyed charades and private acting after dinner, and willingly agreed to bring a more elaborate performance to Rockingham at the end of 1849. At the same time, Bulwer Lytton proposed a 'Dramatic Festival' at his own stately home, Knebworth, which he had inherited from his aristocratic mother. Rehearsals began at Miss Kelly's theatre, but Kate, who was to have taken a small part in a farce, fell through a trapdoor on the stage, and sprained her ankle so severely that her place had to be taken by Mrs Lemon. Georgina participated more successfully–she covered herself with glory, in Dickens' eyes. His own success was professionally observed: 'Ah, sir', said Miss Kelly's master carpenter, 'it's a universal observation in the profession, sir, that it was a great loss to the public when you took to writing books!' Dickens wryly wondered whether the public which was then buying *David Copperfield* by the thousand would agree.

At Knebworth a transportable theatre was installed, and the company triumphed for three nights in succession. 'Dukes and Duchesses'–or at any rate the county gentry of Hertfordshire–patronised the festival. Bulwer was a charming exotic; he had an angular, beaky face with flaming red hair, and affected oriental costumes and furnishings which seemed strange and extravagant. While the acting proceeded, he and Dickens agreed on a new charitable project which might be financed by the amateurs' public performances. This was a Guild of Literature and Art, which was intended to supply pensions and a sort of college or almshouse for indigent writers and journalists.

Unfortunately, Bulwer forgot to provide a proper meal for the actors after their labours. The first night at Knebworth they suffered ravenous pangs of hunger which were not dispelled by sherry and biscuits. What should they do for the future? Bribe the cook? Lemon suggested that food should be smuggled in and surreptitiously consumed in Douglas Jerrold's room at the top of a tower. This was agreed on; Fred Dickens and Augustus Egg fetched supplies from the village, and in 'a stifled stampede' the actors hurried from the stage to the tower, on the second night. Bulwer was indignant when he heard of this, but Dickens mollified him, and he provided a sumptuous meal on the last night.

The transportable theatre constructed at Knebworth could not be erected under the lower ceilings at Rockingham. Dickens supervised fresh stage carpentry there, and Kate was at last able to act again. But her performance and Georgina's were overlooked by Dickens in his delight at the acting of a cousin of the Watsons, the Honourable Mary Boyle. Mary was a tiny, lively, intelligent woman, with blonde hair and big alert eyes, who enjoyed a prolonged flirtation with Dickens. He continued to write to her for the rest of his life, the names they had taken in the farce *Used Up* being their nicknames for each other–'Dearest Meery', and her 'Joe'. He took to sending her to bed

Left:
'Dearest Meery' and her 'Joe' : Mary Boyle and Dickens acting in Used Up.
Left, below:
Mark Lemon as Falstaff.
Right, above:
Macready, the professional actor of the Dickens circle.
Right, below:
Douglas Jerrold, another friend who was willing to act.

with a chaste goodnight kiss while they were staying in the same house, and she began a practice of supplying the flowers for his elaborate buttonholes.

In the world outside, the Great Exhibition in Hyde Park was preparing, and Joseph Paxton privately conducted Dickens round his magnificent Crystal Palace. Macready had decided to retire, and Dickens witnessed his last appearance in *Macbeth*. Afterwards Dickens was the principal speaker at a farewell dinner attended by the aged Charles Kemble, brother of Mrs Siddons.

The exhibition year was to see a round of public performances intended to raise money for the Guild of Literature and Art. Bulwer Lytton had written a new comedy for the amateurs entitled *Not So Bad as We Seem* ('But a great deal worse than we ought to be', was Douglas Jerrold's comment).

Wilkie Collins, the young novelist Dickens was beginning to take under his wing, was brought into the company, and rehearsals began at Covent Garden. The performance itself had to be postponed following the death of Dickens' father and of his infant daughter Dora Annie. The news of the child's death came while Dickens was presiding at the dinner of the General Theatrical Fund. Forster waited until Dickens had given his speech before telling him what had happened, and then took a letter from him to Kate who was convalescing at Malvern. Mark Lemon sat up all night with him beside the body, and Dickens broke the news very gently to Kate before taking her away to Broadstairs where they gradually came to accept the loss of their child.

On their return, rehearsals began again at Devonshire House, which the Duke of Devonshire had lent for the production. The Queen attended the triumphant opening, and saw Dickens emulate his old idol Charles Mathews, taking six successive parts in a farce written by himself and Mark Lemon. A hectic tour of the provinces filled the summer.

'A perfect array of carpenters, gas men, tailors, barbers, property-men, dressers, and servants' accompanied the actors, and after successful performances, civic dignitaries were invited back to cast dinners at which they must have been amazed to see the distinguished literary actors relieving their spirits with wild games of leap-frog around the dinner tables. The tour was a success, but the Guild was a failure. Its charter of incorporation froze its funds for seven years, and by the time they could be used public interest had waned.

Throughout the eighteen-fifties Dickens directed

his children in annual Twelfth Night theatricals. At first they performed hilarious extravaganzas, but as they grew older they were able to put on melodramas like Wilkie Collins' *The Frozen Deep* in their school-room, and when Douglas Jerrold died in 1857 it was this play which Dickens chose for public benefit per-formances to help his widow and children. Queen Victoria attended a special performance, and in spite of her preference for early bed was so entertained that she determined to stay on after the main piece and watch the farce as well. She sent for Dickens during the interval, but with his touchy sense of his own dignity he refused to be presented in his farce costume and makeup. The Queen always had difficulty in con-tacting Dickens, who was somewhat republican-minded in these days: earlier he had refused to act privately for her at Buckingham Palace, as he feared that his daughters might not be treated with the due respect he demanded at Court.

When *The Frozen Deep* went on tour to Man-chester, professional actresses were engaged to take the women's parts. Now it was that the eighteen-year-old actress Ellen Ternan attracted Dickens' attention, and he became infatuated with her. He told Miss Coutts how much impressed he had been by Ellen's 'womanly tenderness', which seems to have surprised him in a girl of her profession.

'I told her on the last night that I was sure she had one of the most genuine and feeling hearts in the world; and I don't think I ever saw anything more prettily simple and unaffected. Yet I remember her on the stage, a little child, and I daresay she was born in a country theatre.'

She doesn't seem to have been a strikingly good actress; *The Frozen Deep* moved her so profoundly while she was on stage that she sobbed unrestrainedly, and the other actors were forced either to share her distress or to distract their attention from their own parts to try to soothe her.

When the tour was over Dickens went on holiday to the Lakes with Wilkie Collins, hoping to find some relief for his aching .love for the young girl. But the holiday only served his public life–it was written up as *The Lazy Tour of Two Idle Apprentices*–and on his return home Dickens moved his bed out of Kate's room into his dressing room, and had the door between the two boarded up.

The decade of frenzied public theatricals may have distracted Dickens' attention from increasing private unhappiness. Henceforth he was to fulfill his need for an immediate audience by public readings from his own works, and when his love for Ellen Ternan brought his relations with Kate to the point of crisis, he began to conduct his private life in an astonishing blaze of self-created and unchivalrous publicity.

The Search for Perfect Love

Ellen Ternan.

Poor Kate Dickens! after twenty-two years of marriage her husband was describing her as 'the only person I have ever known with whom I could not get on'. Repeated childbearing had coarsened her once voluptuous figure. Her face was weighted with depression, a condition her husband either criticised– 'Neither can she get on with herself, or be anything but unhappy'– or cavalierly dismissed as 'a mental disorder under which she sometimes labours'. Fear of the volatile Charles' irritability led the poor lady to worsen her condition by withdrawing ever more nervously into herself; her only outward sign of heeding his upbraiding was an increase in clumsiness and awkwardness which he treated with a hilarity that seems to have masked his true exasperation. He had laughed till the tears ran down his face at the dinner-table where Kate, incredibly, dropped her bracelets in her soup. He snorted at the ankle she sprained while rehearsing at Miss Kelly's theatre. And all the while he noticed that she no longer managed his house-keeping, no longer made herself primarily responsible for the children, and was no longer the obvious person in his entourage who put his own needs first and before all other considerations. These duties had been quietly taken over by the younger, healthier, livelier Georgina, whose girlish admiration for her brother-in-law was not subjected to the stresses of marriage, and whose energies were unchallenged by child-bearing.

If Kate's place in the home was quietly and innocently usurped by Georgina, her place in Dickens' heart was even more gravely at risk. Ever since Mary Hogarth's death Kate had been unable to compete with that idealised memory. Now any pretty, innocent naive little girl might hope to kindle a spark of passion in Dickens that his heavy, gloomy wife could not satisfy, and that was different again from the com-

radely esteem in which he held Georgina and the witty flirt Mary Boyle. A story that one of the Dickens children, seeing Charles preoccupied at the breakfast table, remarked to a visitor, 'poor Papa is in love again', is probably untrue. It is unlikely that such an impertinence would have been ventured in the Dickens household. But the story's long currency testifies to the attraction passing women often had for Dickens, although it should be stressed that his relations with them were almost always innocent; that further story that he allowed Wilkie Collins to take him on lascivious tours among the harlotry of Paris rests on the very uncertain evidence of two jocular letters in which Dickens was probably proposing nothing more than (say) visits to rather 'low' theatres or taverns and his habitual long night walks through disreputable streets.

'Poor Papa' found his first extra-marital love in 1844. He had gone to Liverpool to take the chair at a special *soirée* of the Mechanics Institute. His arrival and reception were something of a personal triumph (not that he was unused to spectacular public ovations) and he was particularly pleased by the bewilderment his dashing 'magpie' waistcoat in black and white caused the audience. Working men's education was a democratic cause, and Dickens brought the house down in his speech by quoting his friend Tennyson's recently written lines:

'Tis only noble to be good–
Kind hearts are more than coronets
And simple faith than Norman blood.

After his long speech Dickens had to introduce an entertainment by local amateurs. He was amused to find that a Miss Christiana *Weller* was to play a piano solo, and in introducing her claimed to have 'some difficulty and tenderness in announcing' her name. The audience was by now eating out of his hand and roared with laughter at this feeble reference to *Pickwick*. Then it was that Dickens' eye caught a pale, beautiful, eighteen-year-old girl in a green fur-trimmed dress who was covered with confusion and cast him a beseeching look as she walked nervously towards the piano where she was to play. Horrified lest his tactless jest might seriously have discomposed the delicate performer, Dickens hurried over to her and led her to the piano, whispering apologetically that he hoped one day she would change her name and be very happy. The girl's solo was a success and should have ended the incident. But back in his hotel that night Dickens was haunted by the memory of a pale delicate face above a green dress trimmed with fur.

The next day Dickens wrote her a brief letter of congratulation on her performance in which he used a tone of strangely intimate personal patronage: 'I felt a pride in you which I cannot express'. He rapidly contrived to meet the girl's family and lunched with Christina and her father to whom he introduced a friend of his own, J. J. Thompson, a fastidious dilettante who lived on a small legacy. Dickens wrote two horribly arch verses for Christiana's album.

I put in a book once, by hook or by crook
The whole race (as I thought) of a 'feller'
Who happily pleased, the town's taste much diseased
And the name of this person was Weller.

I found to my cost that one Weller I lost
Cruel Destiny so to arrange it!
I love her dear name which has won me some fame
But Great Heaven! how gladly I'd change it.

Apart from having a wife to prevent him from changing Christiana's name, Dickens had another speaking engagement in Birmingham which took him away from Liverpool and soon he was back at home in London with Kate and the (by then) five children. But he sent Christiana as a present two volumes of Tennyson's poems which he had received from the poet himself; these he carefully inscribed to her, marking out the poems he preferred at the same time. He also confessed in private letters to Thompson that 'interest in her (spiritual young creature that she is and destined to an early death I fear) has become a sentiment with me'. He knew his position as a successful thirty-two-year-old Victorian paterfamilias made his love ridiculous–'Good God,' he said, 'what a madman I should seem if the incredible feeling I have conceived for that girl could be made plain to anyone'. A curious twist was given to these events when Thompson declared that he too had fallen in love with Christiana. 'I felt the blood go from my face to I don't know where, and my very lips turn white', announced Dickens dramatically: 'I never in my life . . . had the whole current of my life so stopped for the instant as

A fashion print of the sixties, showing the unwieldy size of the crinoline, a fashion which emphasied women's supposed remoteness and modesty.

when I felt at a glance what your letter said'. For Thompson was free to marry Christiana as Dickens was not. Still, better that she should marry Thompson and remain within the orbit of the Dickens circle than that she die a pathetic Victorian death. 'I could better bear her passing,' said Dickens, '*from my arms* to Heaven than I could endure the thought of coldly passing into the world again to see her no more.' Happily, great morbid events need not repeat themselves, and after Mary Hogarth's death Dickens never again had the exquisitely perverse pleasure of innocently embracing a young lady while she died. Christiana lived and flourished, and with Dickens' help and blessing married Thompson. She did not die; she brought up healthy boisterous children in homes on the continent which Dickens found deplorably bohemian when he visited them. Dickens' brother Fred later married Christiana's sister Anna, but the marriage was not happy, and although he was willing to gossip rather unpleasantly about the Thompsons in subsequent years, Dickens really lost touch with and interest in them. The unpleasant gossip about Thompson's mistreatment of Christiana which he repeated to the De la Rues appears, embroidered a little, in *Little Dorrit*, where the triangle of Clennam,

Gowan, and Pet Meagles seems to echo the relations of Dickens, Thompson and Christiana.

Little Dorrit also contains 'poor papa's' fictional comment on his most absurd amorous adventure. When Arthur Clennam meets his boyhood sweetheart Flora Finching after twenty years abroad, Dickens is writing out of his own life.

> Flora, always tall, had grown to be very broad too, and short of breath; but that was not much. Flora, whom he had left a lily, had become a peony; but that was not much. Flora, who had seemed enchanting in all she said and thought, was diffuse and silly. That was much. Flora, who had been spoiled and artless long ago, was determined to be spoiled and artless now. That was a fatal blow!

This is Flora!

> ' "I am sure," giggled Flora, tossing her head with a caricature of her girlish manner, such as a mummy might have presented at her own funeral, if she had lived and died in classical antiquity, "I am ashamed to see Mr Clennam, I am a mere fright, I know he'll find me fearfully changed, I am actually an old woman, it's shocking to be so found out, it's really shocking!"

This is Flora? No, this is Maria!

On 10 February 1855 an innocent letter in the post heralded the return of Maria Beadnell into Dickens' life. He recognised the handwriting and 'three or four and twenty years vanished like a dream'. He was about to go for a week's holiday in Paris with Wilkie Collins, but before he left he wrote directly to Maria giving her his forwarding addresses in France, asking if there were any commissions he could undertake for her there, assuring her that he remembered the past as a 'spring in which I was either more wise or much more foolish than I am now', and insisting that they must meet on his return.

Maria had told him that she was now Mrs Winter, the mother of two little girls. Her husband was a merchant, and she herself was now 'toothless, fat, old and ugly'. Dickens refused to believe this. They exchanged letters while he was in Paris: she appears to have told him that she had really loved him in their youth, and he poured out to her passionate memories of the past and told her how he had treasured every recollection of her. They arranged to meet again on his return to London and they agreed on an elaborate plan which would enable them to meet clandestinely without Kate or Mr Winter being present. Dickens told Maria exactly when to call at his house and ask for Kate, who would be out, so that he could have her sent up to see him alone. His passion for the teasing young girl was totally reawakened, and he spoke of the loss of her as something which could hardly be repaid by his subsequent fame and fortune. 'You ask me to treasure what you tell me, in my heart of hearts', he wrote. 'O see what I have cherished there, through all this time and all these changes!' And there can be

little doubt that he anticipated a consummated love affair as the outcome of this renewed acquaintance. 'Remember', he adjured her as he prepared for their passionate reunion, 'I accept with my whole soul, and reciprocate all'.

The meeting was, of course, a disaster. Maria was indeed old, fat and ugly. The coquettish mannerisms which had charmed in the body of a young girl were grotesque when affected by a stout red-faced matron. Undignified giggling over the past was not something for which Dickens was prepared. And he sensed, too, that Maria herself was disappointed in him. All wishes for an adulterous liaison vanished the moment she appeared and it was embarrassing for Dickens to contemplate a forthcoming family dinner with her husband. Maria herself may have found her acquaintance with England's leading novelist socially prestigious, but her hope of finding a passionate and gifted lover in middle age was cruelly disappointed. When the Winters and the Dickenses did dine together formally, Maria babbled and tittered at Dickens' side throughout the meal and passed on to him the heavy cold which had made her lumpish girlishness even more ridiculous than usual.

Over the next few weeks he slowly tried to break out of the entanglement. He was out whenever she called; he was compelled to accept one invitation to visit her, where he noticed with distaste that she now liked to slip a little brandy into her tea. He persuaded her that his life was too busy to allow him to go on seeing her regularly, and at length managed more or less to sever the connection. But the burst illusion pained him deeply and made it difficult for him to concentrate on his work for some time, while his instant and intense reaction to hearing from Maria in the first place had shown clearly the extent of his dissatisfaction with home life and his desperate inner need to escape out of himself and the reality of his existence into an ideal love affair.

It is hard to say how much Kate knew of all these goings on. Dickens told her nothing about Christiana Weller, and Maria Winter was obviously as disadvantaged by age and even more handicapped by stupidity than she was herself. She may have been jealous of lively Mary Boyle, whose long private walks with her husband might well have aroused indignation in any wife. But after Madame De la Rue she never ventured to offend her husband by displaying public hostility of any of the women in his life. Even when Ellen Ternan brought her marriage crashing down in ruins Kate made no more public protests.

The Marriage Collapses

There is a strange air of romantic fantasy about Dickens' passion for Ellen Ternan in 1857. 'I wish I had been born in the days of Ogres and Dragon-guarded Castles', he wrote to a friend while he was on the *Lazy Tour* holiday with Collins. 'I wish an Ogre with seven heads (and no particular evidence of brains in the whole of them) had taken the Princess whom I adore–you have no idea how intensely I love her!–to this stronghold on the top of a high series of mountains, and there tied her up by the hair. Nothing would suit me half as well this day, as climbing after her, sword in hand, and either winning her or being killed.–*There's* a frame of mind for you, in 1857.' And yet he took no advantage of the opportunity he had to prolong his stay at Doncaster for one day in order to watch the Ternan family's benefit performance at the theatre. His love for Ellen was so strongly based on his belief in her immaculate innocence and purity that he seems to have been afraid of sullying it by any overt approach. Instead, he eased his feelings by writing to his friends of her perfection, and ordered a bracelet for Ellen, just as he always ordered presents for actors and actresses who had worked with his amateur company.

Then disaster fell. The jeweller sent the bracelet to Tavistock House by mistake, and it fell into Kate's hands. Added to Charles' withdrawal from her bedroom this was too much! She reproached and up-braided her husband, who in turn was outraged that such vile aspersions should be cast on his idealised love. In the recriminations which followed Kate soon lost her position of injured strength as Charles accused her of dirty-minded and malicious slander, and demanded that she publicly proclaim her belief in Ellen's innocence by paying the little actress a visit. Katey overheard sobbing in her mother's bedroom and

went in, to be told of this unreasonable order. 'You shall not go', cried Katey, stamping her foot. But Kate lacked the strength to resist her husband's imperious command and she went.

Nevertheless it was clear that breaking point had been reached. Mrs Hogarth and Kate's youngest sister Helen, who had never really liked Charles, were understandably appalled by the humiliation imposed on her. It was they who suggested to her that she should ask for a separation.

If they hoped that this would bring Dickens to his senses they made a grave miscalculation. He leaped at the proposal and immediately opened negotiations to decide on the details. At Kate's request Mark Lemon generously acted for her while Forster represented Dickens. These two considered a variety of proposals: perhaps Kate could continue to act as hostess when Charles entertained and appear with him in public life while actually living separately? Or maybe the two could shuttle between Gad's Hill and Tavistock House, neither ever living in the same place at the same time? Kate rejected both these ideas, which would obviously have been inconvenient as well as undignified. The final agreement was that she should move to a little house on the edge of Camden Town with an income of six hundred pounds a year from Charles and with Charley as her companion. This did not mean that he would be her partisan: 'Don't suppose', he pleaded with his father, 'that in making

Above:
Kate Dickens in middle age.

Right:
Victorian bric-a-brac, fussy and over-decorated, covered all available surfaces in most households and did not make housekeeping any easier.

my choice, I was actuated by any preference for my mother to you. God knows I love you dearly, and it will be a hard day for me when I have to part from you and the girls.' No wonder poor Kate now passed whole days in weeping.

While the negotiations dragged on into 1858 Dickens moved into a small apartment at the *Household Words* office from which he wrote desperately to friends who deplored his conduct. Katie was to call her father 'a wicked man—a very wicked man' in his treatment of her mother, and this hardly seems too strong a description of the man who could deliberately blacken his faithful and long-suffering wife's character, and tell all her remaining friends that she had been and still was a cold and unloving mother.

'Mary and Katie', he told Miss Coutts, 'harden into stone figures of girls when they can be got to go near her, and have their hearts shut up in her presence as if they were closed by some horrid spring. No-one can understand this but Georgina, who has seen it grow from year to year, and who is the best, the most unselfish, and most devoted of human Creatures. Her sister Mary, who died suddenly and who lived with us before her, understood it as well in the first month of our marriage. It is her misery to live in some fatal atmosphere which slays everyone to whom she should be dearest.' The children confirmed that by the eighteen-fifties Kate's depression made her remote and inaccessible. But the suggestion that Mary Hogarth had ever found her sister unloving can only be regarded as a blatant lie. That Dickens should utter it with such passionate conviction gives some indication of the misery he suffered—Katey said he was like a madman—while the fantasy of his love life destroyed the remaining peace of his family life.

Just as the negotiations were almost complete a report reached Dickens' ears which led him to threaten cutting Kate off without a penny. Mrs Hogarth and Helen had been explaining the separation to their friends as the result of Dickens' adultery. The fair name of Ellen Ternan was being publicly besmirched, and in a violent fury Dickens demanded that this claim be retracted. The gossips seemed to have been unconvinced by Dickens' vehement declarations of innocence; matters were at a standstill for a fortnight before the Hogarths could be persuaded to put their names to a document declaring that 'we now disbelieve such statements. We know that they are not believed by Mrs Dickens, and we pledge ourselves on all occasions to contradict them as entirely destitute of foundation.' With this weapon in his hands Dickens carried his campaign for the proclamation of Ellen's virtue into the press. He drew up a statement of his own claiming that 'some domestic trouble of long standing of a sacredly private nature' had been made 'the occasion of misrepresentations, most grossly false, most monstrous and most cruel, involving not only me, but innocent persons dear to my heart, and innocent persons of whom I have no knowledge, if indeed they have any existence.'

'Innocent persons' rather than 'an innocent person' was used because slander had touched Georgina as well as Ellen. Georgina admired her brother-in-law and had no prospect of a career or security outside his house. She believed that she was doing useful work as his housekeeper and to her mother's amazement she refused to go into exile with Kate. Although her action went some way to convince a few people that Dickens' honour must be as bright as he claimed, others gloated over the possibility that Kate's own sister might be the disruptive mistress who had led to the separation. Such a liaison would have been incestuous both in law and in general opinion at the time, so that Dickens may have felt compelled to take public steps to clear the name of the sister-in-law who had courageously accepted an equivocal position on his behalf. 'I most solemnly declare', he concluded his statement, 'that all the lately whispered rumours touching the trouble at which I have glanced, are abominably false. And that whosoever repeats one of them after this denial will lie as wilfully and as foully as it is possible for any false witness to lie before Heaven and earth.'

Forster sensibly told him that he could not possibly publish such a statement. Mark Lemon categorically refused to print it in *Punch*. Dickens agreed to abide by the decision of the editor of the *Times* who foolishly told him to go ahead and send it to the newspapers. And so a totally private matter, which might have been the substance of a little gossip in literary circles, was thrown open to the public.

Of course Dickens' statement made things worse rather than better. It was so vaguely worded that many readers had no idea what it was they were being told. Across the Atlantic Dickens' friends were perturbed by the garbled stories which reached them. In the silliest action of his career Dickens wrote another statement, a fuller and more elaborate one which was to be circulated privately among those of his distant acquaintances who were still dissatisfied. This found its way into the press, and what had formerly been known mysteriously as 'some domestic trouble', was now generally revealed as a complete marital breakdown and separation. Worse still, this letter, which should never have been printed, made specific charges against Kate. 'In the manly consideration towards Mrs Dickens which I owe my wife', Dickens had written, 'I will merely remark that the peculiarity of her character has thrown all the children on someone else.' Helen and Mrs Hogarth became 'two wicked persons who should have spoken very differently of me, in consideration of earned respect and gratitude'. Ellen's name was still concealed. She became 'a young lady for whom I have great attachment and regard. Upon my soul and honour there is not on this earth a more virtuous and spotless creature than that young lady. I know her to be innocent and pure and as good as my own dear daughters. I will not repeat her name—I honour it too much'.

This was a bombshell for the thousands of readers who saw Dickens as the laureate of hearth and home,

FINELADYISM.

First Elegant Mamma. "HOW SHOCKING THIS IS!—THE WAY NURSERYMAIDS NEGLECT THE CHILDREN!"

Second Do. "YES, DEAR! AND I DON'T SEE THAT ANYTHING CAN BE DONE. FOR WHAT WITH PARTIES, AND THE TIME ONE NATURALLY DEVOTES TO DRESSING, AND THE NUMEROUS CALLS ONE HAS TO MAKE, ONE CAN'T LOOK AFTER ONE'S OWN CHILDREN, YOU KNOW!"

the philosopher of Christmas who had persuaded Victorian England that family ties and cosy domestic junketings were among the highest blessings to be found in a Christian nation. The newspapers observed that it was a grave mistake for Dickens to tell readers 'how little, after all, he thinks of the marriage tie'. The heavy blame thrown on Kate was rightly castigated in the press: 'This favourite of the public informs some hundreds of thousands of readers that the wife whom he was vowed to love and cherish had utterly failed to discharge the duties of a mother; and he further hints that her mind is disordered. If this is "manly consideration", we should like to be favoured with a definition of unmanly selfishness and heartlessness.' Nor did the protestations of innocence cut much ice; '*Qui s'excuse, s'accuse*', was one dry comment. It was with some trepidation that Forster watched the sales of the new journal *All the Year Round* for signs that self-created scandal might have shaken Dickens' popularity.

It was a relief to everyone that it had not—it would have been of no advantage to Kate to watch her husband's earning power dry up as she remained dependent on him.

Dickens found his nine children something of a burden, and the huge Victorian family proved tiresome to many middle-class parents. Cartoon by John Leech from Punch.

91

Kate received general credit for her dignified silence. This was probably less a matter of considered policy than the dictate of her inactive temperament. For a short time Charley's presence and sympathy was a consolation to her, but soon he too had left her, as business called him to the Far East. She was brutally excluded from the remainder of her husband's life; she was not a guest at Katey's wedding, and she received the coolest acknowledgements to her letter of sympathy when Walter's death in India was reported. She continued to read Charles' novels as they came out, and she clung hopelessly to her letters which, as she said, would show the world that he had indeed loved her once.

Charles was now free of Kate's presence, though there was no question of his marrying Ellen. Divorce had never entered his mind, either because this would have been a move which might seriously have damaged his sales, or because, like the majority of middle-class English men at the time, he did not approve of it.

Furthermore, he had no grounds for divorcing Kate (adultery was the only cause for which a wife might be divorced and Kate had been unquestionably faithfull) and although she could possibly have accused him of cruelty or desertion, he was not a man who would meekly accept the role of guilty party when he believed himself totally innocent, even with an expedient end in view.

So for the rest of his life Dickens was without a wife. Georgina, whose domestic virtues had been celebrated in the pair of household heroines of his middle novels—Agnes in *David Copperfield* and Esther Summerson in *Bleak House*—became his housekeeper and oversaw the upbringing of the youngest children, Harry and Plorn. For some time Dickens kept a discreet fatherly eye on Ellen. Her elder sister Fanny married his friend Tom Trollope, brother of the novelist, and Dickens, who had probably known the family for a considerable period of time, advised Mrs Ternan on the education and careers of her daughters. At the end of 1858 Ellen and her younger sister Fanny were living in lodgings in Berners Street off Oxford Street, and here Dickens helped them when an officious policeman called to enquire about the two young girls. Whether the constable suspected them of being in moral danger, living alone, or whether, as Dickens suspected, he had been bribed by a libidinous 'swell' to establish contact with these supposedly 'loose' actresses, cannot now be determined. But Dickens made a complaint to Scotland Yard on their behalf (it was the only occasion on which he criticised the police), and it must have been some years before Ellen actually became his mistress.

Left:
Tavistock House, Dickens' London home from 1851 till 1860.

Right:
Girl at the Waterfall – *a picture of Georgina by Maclise.*

THE WATERFALL, ST. NIGHTON'S KIEVE, NEAR TINTAGEL.   SIGNED AND DATED 1842   BY DANIEL MACLISE, R.A. (b.1806, d.1870).   No.F. 22.

'So Many Children'

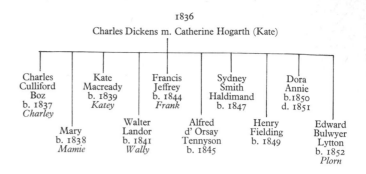

1836
Charles Dickens m. Catherine Hogarth (Kate)

Charles Culliford Boz b. 1837 *Charley*

Mary b. 1838 *Mamie*

Kate Macready b. 1839 *Katey*

Walter Landor b. 1841 *Wally*

Francis Jeffrey b. 1844 *Frank*

Alfred d' Orsay Tennyson b. 1845

Sydney Smith Haldimand b. 1847

Henry Fielding b. 1849

Dora Annie b.1850 d. 1851

Edward Bulwyer Lytton b. 1852 *Plorn*

By 1851 Dickens was again looking for a new house. Although Devonshire Terrace had proved capacious by comparison with Doughty Street, it was hardly large enough for the ever-increasing brood of Dickens children. The latter part of his life was so taken up with concern for the careers of his offspring, and his happiness was so clouded by his 'having so many children by a wife who was totally uncongenial', as one of his friends noted, that his parental life deserves serious consideration in spite of its having had little obvious effect on his fiction.

Kate bore Charles ten children in all, of whom only Dora Annie (1850-1) died in infancy, though there were in addition two miscarriages. Dickens made no secret of the fact that the size of his family was a burden to him. He facetiously suggested 'a little service in St Paul's beseeching that I may be considered to have done enough towards my country's population'. The last child was explicitly unwelcomed in 1852: 'My wife', he wrote, is quite well again, after favouring me (I think I could have dispensed with the compliment) with No. 10.' It could of course be laughed off: the pregnant Kate could be accused of 'conducting an anti-Malthusian experiment', or a correspondent who asked after his children would be told: 'I have laid down my pen and taken a long breath after writing this family history. I have also considered whether there are any more children, and I don't think there are. If I should remember two or three others presently, I will mention them in a postscript' (He had in fact forgotten one). Lord Jeffrey saw fit to admonish him gently and included some much needed sympathy for Kate: 'There can never be too many Dickenses in the world,' he wrote, 'but these *overbearings* exhaust the parent tree.' They seem indeed to have exhausted Kate, whose natural placidity developed into a torpid

lassitude, and who, one suspects, was subject to recurrent post-natal depressions which must have been intensified by her husband's total lack of sympathy for her inability to force herself to carry out her household duties. This became a major factor in the Dickenses' marital disharmony, and Charles cannot escape blame for his tendency to treat Kate as if she were solely responsible for the endless flow of children whose conception he had deliberately done nothing to prevent.

Of the nine surviving children only two were girls, Mary ('Mamie') and Kate Macready ('Katey'). The fanciful nicknames Dickens gave them described them accurately enough: Mamie was 'Mild Glo'ster' and seems to have inherited her mother's placid temperament to a degree that has been described as 'almost imbecile amiability'. She never married, never left home, and became, with her Aunt Georgina, the constant domestic companion of her father's last years. She took seriously his injunction to his children to preserve his good name as their best inheritance, and with Georgina published a selection of his letters after his death 'with a view of showing him in his homely, domestic life—of showing how in the midst of his own constant and arduous work, no household matter was considered too trivial to claim his care and attention'. Mamie even seems to have tried to improve on the memory of her father's taste, claiming that he liked her to play Chopin, Mozart and Mendelssohn on the piano, whereas no one else remembers his taste venturing much higher than popular ballads.

Katey was 'Lucifer Box', and with her fiery artistic nature seems the only one of Dickens' children to have inherited something of his own vigorous personality. When her parents separated she alone showed any inclination to take her mother's side, and soon afterwards she married Charles Collins, Wilkie's brother, the artist, with the apparent intention of establishing her independence of her father. This at any rate was how Dickens interpreted her action, as Mamie found him after the wedding weeping in the bride's abandoned dress and saying, 'But for me Katey would not have left home.' Katey was almost the only near relative who refused to sponge off Dickens. Although Collins was not a particularly successful painter and she herself achieved little in spite of her art training at Bedford College, she never asked her father for money, and succeeded in creating a tasteful late Victorian home for herself and her husband on limited means.

Charley, the eldest boy, ('the Slodgering Blee' or 'Flaster Floby') was less spirited and independent. As a child his sensitive nature and tendency to 'fade' in company caused Dickens some concern. He was educated with his next brother Walter at Joseph Charles King's private school in St John's Wood, an excellent school attended by the Macready boys, where Latin and Greek were made colourful and exciting and, unusually for the period, King's daughter helped with the teaching. (In all other respects she was quite unlike Miss Cornelia Blimber, the dry and sandy lady who contributes to the dull classics teaching at her father's cramming school in *Dombey and Son*; she later contributed some very syrupy pieces to *Household Words*). Miss Coutts undertood to pay for Charley's education, and at her insistence he was sent to Eton where Dickens was delighted to find that he was popular with the other boys and highly regarded by his tutor. Dickens enjoyed taking Charley and his schoolfriends on jolly picnic outings on the river where he plied them with champagne and hoped they would nevertheless return to school sober. But the tolerant atmosphere of Eton under its humane headmaster Hawtrey seemed to encourage a fatal lack of perseverence in Charley. He never achieved real excellence in his studies and Dickens was quite content to remove him from school when he was fifteen and allow the boy to embark on the business career he had chosen for himself. After a short period in Germany Charley joined the staff of Baring's bank and later set up in business on his own, visiting China and the Orient in 1860 to purchase a large consignment of tea with which he hoped to establish himself as an importer. Lack of perseverance rather than business strategy probably dictated his diversification into paper milling, and the failure of his mill, with his ensuing bankruptcy for £1,000 in 1868, distressed his father gravely. A job was found for Charley in the office of *All the Year Round*, where he proved useful and reasonably efficient. This led to the magazine's being made over to him after his father's death, and he edited it with reasonable success though little flair for some years. This could be combined with publishing–to his father's distress he had married Bessie Evans, after Dickens had broken with Bradbury and Evans–and Charley's later career was not so chequered as those of some of his brothers.

Walter Landor ('Young Skull' from his high cheek bones) went from Mr King's to a military coach, as Miss Coutts' influence could be used to gain commissions for the boys if they were willing to go into the services. From here he went to Brackenbury and Wynn's school at Wimbledon, which was attended by most of his younger brothers, and in 1857 he became a cadet in the Indian Army. He was promoted lieutenant during the mutiny but six years later he died in Calcutta and Dickens' distress was aggravated by the receipt of claims for debts in excess of a hundred and forty pounds from his regiment. One bill might have amused the writer in less depressing circumstances :

Humble petition of Gunga Rum Cloth
Most humbly sheweth
I most humbly beg to write these few humble lines
to your great honour
        –Honoured Sir–
Your poor petitioner is want 14 Re 8 ans.
from April 1862
   And he havnt paid to me yet and Sir
I have heard now Dickens is gone to England some
   days ago
   And Sir now I will get these Re with your kind
Should I be so fortunate as to succeed my request
   for which
Act of generosity I shall ever pray for your long
   life and prosperity.

Walter the cadet.

The next boy, Francis Jeffrey ('Chickenstalker'), was also destined for the East. He had been educated at an English school in Boulogne to which several of the boys were sent as continental education was cheap, and then had been brought home for the bar. But he suffered from a crippling stammer which Dickens was unable to cure by taking him through readings of Shakespeare, and it was soon clear that a professional career was out of the question. A business partnership with Charley was mooted but turned down, and after Frank had failed to prove his worth in the *All the Year Round* office, and failed to get into the Foreign Office, he was sent off to join the Bengal Mounted Police. He was not particularly successful here, and after his father's death came back to England where he ignored and insulted his family until they were able to despatch him to the Canadian Mounties.

Alfred D'Orsay Tennyson Dickens amused London with his elaborate name. D'Orsay was so scandalous a dandy and Tennyson so respectable a poet that Robert Browning referred to them as the boy's 'godfather and devilfather'. Alfred's education at Boulogne and Wimbledon should have prepared him for the army, but although he was reasonably steady he lacked the ability to succeed in the fair competition which was superseding the purchase of commissions through influence, and after two years in a London office he emigrated to Australia where he made a reasonable success of business and farming.

But his younger brother, Sydney Smith Haldimand, proved one of his father's greatest disappointments. He was long Dickens' favourite son and nicknamed 'The Ocean Spectre' from his Paul Dombey-like habit of gazing out to sea in his infancy. This foible was prophetic; he expressed an early desire to join the navy and was sent from Boulogne to a naval coaching establishment in Southsea, where he passed his examinations successfully and came home, 'All eyes and gold buttons', the tiniest midshipman in the navy. He satisfied the captain when he went to sea and amused his ship mates by buying so much of a coloured bumboat woman's stock that she invited him to visit her on land. This, together with an alarming predilection for collecting ornate golden rings, foreshadowed the reckless extravagance which was to lead to a break between Sydney and his father, when Dickens found yet another of his sons repeatedly asking to be helped with unnecessary debts. By 1870 Sydney had been ordered not to visit his family when he came home on leave, and his untimely death a year after his father's cut short a career which had been promising in spite of his personal failings.

Henry Fielding Dickens was the only real success in the family. He alone recognised that changing times called for more education than Dickens was normally prepared to provide for his sons, and after a highly successful school career at Boulogne and Wimbledon he insisted on going to Trinity Hall, Cambridge and reading law. Dickens mistrusted universities, which he regarded as oldfashioned places where young men were encouraged to be indolent and extravagant, but Henry justified his choice of a career by winning a college scholarship, to his father's enormous satisfaction. He would have been even more satisfied had he survived to see Henry go on to a successful legal career and a knighthood.

The greatest disappointment of all was the youngest child, Edward Bulwer Lytton Dickens. Although he had been unwelcomed when he was born he rapidly became the family favourite, and was given the most elaborate of all the flamboyant nicknames Dickens made up for his children—Plornishmaroontigoonter. 'Plorn' stuck as a nickname till an age at which the other children had reverted to their given names. The boy was petted and adored by his father, though not apparently spoilt; Dickens was too much the domestic martinet to spoil any of his sons. But Plorn gave problems. He was only six when his parents separated—indeed, Dickens had by then packed so many sons off into early careers that only Harry and Plorn, nine and six years old respectively, had to stay with Georgina and the girls in the miserable house. Yet the upheaval did not affect Harry's career adversely, and Plorn, who had been very close to him as a boy, was to resent his brother's success deeply when he reached manhood.

It was difficult at first to find a school that Plorn would accept. He was, according to Dickens, 'sensitive and shy' and found Wimbledon 'confusingly large'. As the favourite of his Aunt Georgina as well as his father, Plorn was kept back from Boulogne as long as possible, and seems to have acquired a distaste for all

Alfred D'Orsay Tennyson Dickens.

schooling. His admission that he liked one school he attended was described by his father as 'the great social triumph of modern times', but the thankless task of trying to educate him was not kept up for long: at fourteen he was pulled out of school and sent to the Royal Agricultural College at Cirencester to be prepared for a farming career in Australia. Optimism burned strongly in Dickens: 'By the Lord,' he exclaimed, 'he ought to be a first-rate settler after all his cramming!' Plorn was tearfully shipped off after only six months at Cirencester and for the rest of his father's life—indeed, for the rest of his own life too—led an unsettled, unsatisfactory, debt-ridden life in Australia.

Dickens loved all these difficult children deeply and their fecklessness was a terrible burden to him at the end of his life. 'All his fame goes for nothing', said a friend in conversation, 'since he has not the one thing. He is very unhappy in his children.'

'Nobody can say', came the reply, 'how much too much of this the children have to hear.'

And it was true. Once they reached adolescence the children would be constantly made aware that their father required more of them than they could give; required traces of his own energy, his own methodical approach to life and work, and his own pursuit of success, while somehow also he demanded that they must eradicate the family tendency to extravagant living. It was, of course, hopeless. The sensitive boys, Charley and Plorn, drifted indecisively. The ones who were sent abroad kicked over the traces. And all of them had unhappy memories of childhood in which the demon was not Kate but Charles, the father who had dominated the household and imposed his will on them like a true Victorian martinet.

While the children were very small they could enjoy their father's boisterousness and the elaborate humour which led him to give them fantastic nicknames and address them in a special funny voice for children. At special outings, parties, picnics and festivities too he would always have been fun; one can imagine him saying, like his own Joe Gargery, 'What larks!' Other children, like Thackeray's daughters, who only met the great man at children's parties, saw him as a richly lively host dispensing goodies and performing wonderful conjuring tricks. But the family knew of the daily round of inspection; every child's room must be in apple pie order or there would be trouble; even on holiday one of the boys would be deputed to see that coats, hats and boots were properly put away. Woe betide the child who failed to appear a model.

'He would take as much pains about the hanging of a picture, the choosing of furniture, the superintending of any little improvement in the house, as he would about the more serious business of his life', said Mamie innocently. The other children might have found harsher things to say about the obsessive con-

cern with order which weighed upon their lives.

Still, it would be untrue to suggest that they were a divided or deeply unhappy family. In the big garden at Devonshire Terrace and Gad's Hill Place, the old rose-brick house outside Rochester which Dickens bought in fulfilment of his childhood dream in 1856, they all enjoyed the presence of a sequence of pets: two ravens which were exposed as thieves of family property after they died, Newman Noggs the little pony, and a succession of dogs—Mister Timber Doodle, Mamie's Mister Bouncer, Don and Bumble the Newfoundlands, Linda the St Bernard, Turk the mastiff, and the terrible bloodhound Sultan who attacked first Bouncer, then a whole company of soldiers marching past the house, and finally a little girl, after which he had to be shot.

And like most families the Dickenses could unite against an outsider. Hans Christian Andersen, the Danish fairy tale writer, stayed at Gad's Hill in 1857. He found the family charming and told the children stories in the fields. Goodness knows whether they understood him as he knew next to no English, and very few people in England could understand his attempts at French, Italian and German; his translator even found him incomprehensible in Danish. He travelled from Gad's Hill to London where he lost himself in cabs and was easily terrified by what he regarded as the threatening aspect of the English. On the one occasion he limped into Tavistock House having abandoned a cab which took a route he did not recognise. Fearing that the cab man intended to rob him, Andersen had put his watch and money together with anything else he found in his pockets into his boots before walking home. The girls found him 'a bony bore'. Dickens' friends objected to his childish jokes; Wilkie Collins, for instance, was not pleased to find himself being laughed at by hop pickers near Rochester because Andersen had secretly slipped a daisy chain over his hat. When he went back to Denmark, Dickens left a card on his dressing table reading 'Hans Christian Andersen slept in this room for five weeks which seemed to the family ages.'

Perhaps Dickens' greatest difficulty with his children was a surprising shyness, a difficulty in unbending towards them when they were no longer little. When Plorn left for Australia Dickens completely broke down at the station, and Henry, who was with them, realised for the first time how deeply their father loved his children. And when Henry himself returned home after his first year at Trinity with the exciting news that he had won the best mathematical scholarship in the college, he was deeply disappointed when his father said no more than 'Capital! Capital!' Yet a little later as the two were walking silently home together he turned to his son with tears in his eyes, gripped his hand painfully, and said brokenly, 'God bless you my boy, God bless you.'

Henry Fielding Dickens, called after one of Dickens' favourite novelists.

The Garrick
Club Row

'There is no use denying the matter or blinking it now. I am become a sort of great man in my way—all but at the top of the tree : Indeed there if the truth were known and having a great fight up there with Dickens.' Thus William Makepeace Thackeray to his mother in 1848, when the publication of *Vanity Fair* was at last bringing him success as a writer. Thackeray's early career had been chequered : business, painting, book-illustration and journalism had none of them proved very profitable, and a raffish life in Paris when he was young, together with the failure of an Indian bank, had lost him the independent income he had expected to sustain him as a gentleman. When success came to him he was forever looking over his shoulder at Dickens and wondering uneasily how their work compared. In this he was encouraged by admirers like Charles Kingsley, Charlotte Brontë, George Eliot and Tennyson, who deplored the 'vulgarity' they detected in Dickens' work and tried to persuade Thackeray that he had 'completely beaten Dickens out of the inner circle'.

Thackeray himself, although aware of their rivalry for public esteem, and inclined to be resentful of Dickens' overwhelming commercial success, was too fine and serious a critic of the other's novels not to recognise greatness. But again, he tended to view it competitively, and to be depressed when thinking of Dickens' 'divine genius'. He was astonished by his 'fecundity of imagination', and towards the end of his life admitted to a visitor, 'I am played out. All I can do now is to bring out my old puppets . . . but, if he lived to be ninety, Dickens will still be creating new characters. In his art that man is marvellous.'

This sense of rivalry clouded relations between the two writers. There is little evidence that Dickens felt troubled by Thackeray's rise to fame, but kind friends told Thackeray otherwise. He heard that Dickens could not forgive him for the success of *Vanity Fair*, and this led to constraint between them.

Real trouble only began with Dickens' separation scandal. Thackeray heard 'horrible stories buzzing about' which disturbed him, but his greatest sympathy was for Kate. 'The poor matron,' he wrote privately to his mother, 'after 22 years of marriage going away out of her home—a fatal story for our trade.' This on its own might have done no harm, but going into the Garrick Club one day Thackeray heard members exchanging gossip about the separation really being caused by an affair between Dickens and Georgina.

'No,' said Thackeray in his hearty man-of-the-world manner, 'it's no such thing. It's with an actress.' This was reported back to Dickens who was unreasonably outraged. Thackeray's gauche bluffness in conversation was constantly getting him into difficulties with people who should have recognised his essential good nature. However, the trouble was patched over when Thackeray explained that he had told his story to contradict the other much worse one, though he continued to tell friends plaintively that 'there is some row about an actress in the case and he [Dickens] denies with the utmost infuriation any charge against her or himself.'

The total breach came a year later when Thackeray fell out with a young protegé of Dickens. Edmund Yates was a gossipy popular journalist of small talent who belonged to the somewhat sycophantic circle of young men surrounding Dickens. He had endeared himself to the great man by defending him vehemently in the separation crisis, and like both Dickens and Thackeray he was a member of the Garrick Club, the writers' and journalists' haven of which Thackeray was an enthusiastic founder member.

Edmund Yates.

On a hot June evening Yates came into the office of *Town Talk*, a little weekly gossip sheet for which he worked. He found that a promised article had not arrived and thereupon sat down to write a piece to fill up the vacant space. The previous week he had written a short sketch of Dickens and he now determined to dash off a similar pen portrait of Thackeray. He described Thackeray's appearance, conduct and personality as he knew them from casual contact in the Garrick Club. Thackeray must have snubbed the young man in the past as, according to Yates, his bearing was cold and uninviting, his style of conversation either openly cynical, or affectedly good-natured and benevolent; his *bonhomie* was forced, his wit biting, and his pride easily touched. Worse still, Yates predicted an end to Thackeray's popularity and ventured some crude criticism of his writing : 'There is a want of heart in all he writes, which is not to be balanced by the most brilliant sarcasm and the most perfect knowledge of the working of the human heart.'

When Thackeray read the piece he was stung by its insolence and wrote an indignant reprimand to Yates. 'We meet at a club', he said, 'where, before you were born I believe, I and other gentlemen have been in the habit of talking without any idea that our conversation would supply paragraphs for professional vendors of 'Literary Talk'; and I don't remember that out of that Club I have ever exchanged six words with you.'

He evidently expected an apology but his imperious tone had in turn annoyed Yates, who drafted an angry reply which pointed out, fairly enough, that Thackeray had inserted in his novels many recognisable and insulting caricatures of his friends and acquaintances, including a number of members of the Garrick Club. Before sending this counter-attack, Yates consulted Dickens who told him firmly that his original article was indefensible but agreed that Thackeray's hectoring letter put apology out of the question.

Thackeray referred the matter to the committee of the Garrick Club, suggesting that it would be 'fatal to the comfort of the Club', and 'intolerable in a society of gentlemen', if members were allowed to publish abusive articles about one another. Dickens, as a member of the committee, insisted that this was a private quarrel between two members and had nothing to do with the Club ; Yates, too, urged that while his article might have been in bad taste the committee was 'not a Committee of taste'. But the serious and distinguished assembly of Victorian writers disagreed, and the committee informed Yates that he must 'make an ample apology to Mr Thackeray, or retire from the club'. Dickens thereupon resigned from the committee, while Yates appealed over their heads to a general meeting of all the club members. Thackeray, meanwhile, had written some abusive comments on 'young Grubstreet, who corresponded with three-penny papers', in a number of his novel *The Virginians* which was coming out at the time.

At the general meeting Dickens defended Yates, but failed to persuade his fellow members that it was no business of the club to order an apology. Yates was expelled on his refusal to apologise and on Dickens' advice took counsel's opinion on the legality of the expulsion. With legal backing, he attempted to make an entry into the club's premises, and was forcibly thrown out by the secretary. Dickens now wrote to Thackeray, hoping to save Yates and the club from being dragged through the courts, and asked whether he could not act as a mediator in the dispute. But Thackeray, finding that Dickens had all along been Yates' advisor, wrote back a very cold and formal letter which elicited from Forster an indignant, 'He be damned with his "yours, etc." ' Dickens was even more annoyed when Thackeray quoted his letter to the club, as he had intended it to be an entirely private offer. From then on all friendship between the two novelists ended.

It was not until 1863 that a reconciliation took place. Katey had told Thackeray that her father would certainly respond to any gesture of friendship made to him. Soon after that, while Thackeray was talking to a friend in the hall of the Athenaeum Club, Dickens passed by, without a word, as was his custom on meeting Thackeray. Thackeray suddenly hurried over to him holding out his hand, and said, 'It is time this foolishment estrangement should cease and that we should be to each other what we used to be. Come ; shake hands.' Friendship was restored, although Thackeray could not resist telling Katey, 'Your father knew he was wrong and was full of apologies–.' Katey knew her father better than that, and interrupted him at once, demanding the truth. But it was true that friendship had been restored, and this was a considerable relief to Dickens when Thackeray died suddenly one week later.

Tale-teller of Two Cities : the international fame of Dickens maturity. From a cartoon by Gill.

Public Readings

Mr. CHARLES DICKENS'S READING.

Doors open at half-past 7.
The Audience are respectfully requested to be in their places by 10 minutes to 8 o'clock.

80 ONE SHILLING.

The Reading will last two hours.

Dickens never really regarded himself as a wealthy man. He knew that he was successful, and he knew that his fortune excelled anything that might have been anticipated for the son of a pay clerk. But the great world in which he mixed contained far wealthier members–Bulwer Lytton, for example, had inherited his own huge estate which brought him in an income as well as supplying him with a magnificent home. Compared with Lytton's Knebworth, Gad's Hill Place, the 'big house' with which Dickens had marked his success, was a tiny box. Although he had bought the meadow outside it, and delighted in growing hay as well as garden produce, the master of Gad's Hill was clearly a householder and not a landowner.

By the standards of the time Dickens was but modestly successful, in terms of cash as well as land. The great mid-Victorian capitalists amassed fortunes which far outweighed that of their period's most successful writer. In *Little Dorrit* Dickens created Mr Merdle, financier and swindler, whose corrupt presence at the centre of fashionable society is the means of a far more telling criticism of capitalist industrialism and human avarice than anything attempted earlier. For the details of Merdle's career he had drawn on the lives of two notoriously corrupt business men ; John Sadleir, director of an Irish bank which collapsed when he was found to have forged deeds and railway shares as secure assets against the enormous sums he was drawing in his own name ; and George Hudson, the pushful York tradesman who directed and cooked the books of half the railroads in the country. Neither of these two men ever commanded the respect that Dickens held in intellectual and popular circles, and although, at the height of his power, Hudson was surrounded by aristocratic toadies who hoped he might show them the way to railway wealth, his vulgar

social origin and boorish manners made him unacceptable as Dickens never was in polite society. It is interesting, then, to observe that Sadleir's personal overdraft at the time of his suicide stood at £200,000, while Hudson had appropriated to himself at least £600,000 from the four largest companies under his control. Dickens' spectacular success had made him worth no more than £50,000 or so by the eighteen-fifties, and this seemed to him no more than he needed to maintain himself and his large family. He was not too proud to accept Miss Coutts' offer to pay for Charley's education, and did not feel that he held a sufficient financial surplus to allow him to contribute lavishly to charity.

But if he was not unusually generous with his money beyond his immediate circle he was nonetheless lavish with his time and energy. The amateur theatricals he produced were almost invariably devoted to raising funds for good causes or needy persons. He was never too busy to address public meetings and preside at dinners on behalf of the educational causes he favoured, and in 1853 he agreed to give public readings in Birmingham on behalf of the newly established Working Men's Institute. He read *A Christmas Carol* on 27 December, and followed this with *The Cricket on the Hearth* two days later. The following night he read *Carol* again to an audience of working men whom he had asked to attend at reduced prices. These readings were a great success and led to others on behalf of similar good causes over the next few years. It was in 1857, when he was reading the *Carol* on behalf of the Great Ormond Street Children's Hospital, a charity he greatly admired, that it occurred to him that what succeeded so well for charity might be turned to profit. Forster was dismayed by the suggestion that his friend should undertake a tour of public readings for gain; it would be making an undignified exhibition of himself, unworthy of a man of letters and a gentleman, he felt. But Miss Coutts, although surprised, saw nothing untoward in the project: 'I think upon the whole that most people would be glad you should have the money, rather than other people', she added. Dickens promptly directed his agent to arrange a national tour for himself with appearances in thirty-five or forty places throughout England, which he hoped might be worth £10,000. He added the death scene of Paul Dombey, some Sairey Gamp sketches from *Martin Chuzzlewit*, and the Trial Scene from *Pickwick* to the Christmas stories he had already used, and in August of 1858 he began a reading tour that was to take him from Plymouth to Edinburgh with an interval in Ireland, and which brought him over 3000 guineas clear profit.

The readings were an enormous success. For their subject matter he returned to the boisterous comedy and unrestrained sentiment of his early novels. The novels after *David Copperfield*–*Bleak House*, *Hard Times*, and *Little Dorrit*–had become darker as he challenged the whole structure of his society instead of focussing on simple reversible evils like bad schools or workhouse diets. 'Boz's fun' which had brought him his original audience was less in evidence, and some readers were now indignant with what they saw as the 'sullen socialism' of his new work. Walter Bagehot, the conservative lawyer whose writings exemplify intelligent moderate Victorian middleclass attitudes summed up the readers' sense of a difficult change in Dickens'

social message: 'He began by describing really removable evils in a style which would induce all persons, however, insensible, to remove them if they could; he has ended by describing the natural evils and inevitable pain of the present state of being in such a manner as must tend to excite discontent and repining.'

Dickens was too serious and responsible a writer to meet public criticism by falsifying the truth as he saw it. He knew that the dense and difficult novels of his maturity were as fine as anything he had ever written. Yet he throve on popular adulation and always hoped to meet his readers at their own level. Public reading from his early works with their proven popularity were a way in which he could confront his readers directly. Laughing or weeping faces were an even more reassuring evidence of success than climbing sales figures, and Dickens had a deep inner need to prove to himself that the creations which gave him so much pleasure were a source of delight to others.

At the readings, he laughed and wept with his hearers. A listener in Harrogate '*could not* compose himself at all, but laughed until he sat wiping his eyes with his handkerchief', and 'gave a kind of cry, as if it were too much for him. It was uncommonly droll', said Dickens, 'and made me laugh heartily'. The standing ovations he received helped him to weather the assaults of the newspapers which were attacking his conduct to Kate, and in Scotland he was overwhelmed

An announcement advertising Dickens' programme of readings in Dublin.

MR. CHARLES DICKENS
WILL READ IN THE ROUND ROOM, ROTUNDA, DUBLIN:—
On MONDAY EVENING, AUGUST 23rd, at 8 o'Clock, his
CHRISTMAS CAROL.
On TUESDAY EVENING, AUGUST 24th, at 8 o'Clock, his
CHIMES.
On WEDNESDAY AFTERNOON, AUGUST 25th, at 3 o'Clock, the Story of
LITTLE DOMBEY.
On THURSDAY EVENING, AUGUST 26th, at 8 o'Clock,
THE POOR TRAVELLER,
BOOTS AT THE HOLLY TREE INN, AND MRS. GAMP.
PLACES FOR EACH READING:—Stalls (numbered and reserved) phillings; Unr
Seats, Half-a-Crown; Back Seats, One Shilling.
Tickets to be had of Messrs. McGlashan and Gill, Publishers, &c., 50, Upper Street, Dublin, where a Plan of the Stalls may be seen.
Each Reading will last two hours.
☞ On only one occasion, during Mr. Dickens's experience, some ladies and gentlemen in the Stalls caused great inconvenience and confusion (no doubt, unintentionally), by leaving their places during the last quarter of an hour of the Reading, when the general attention could least bear to be disturbed. This elicited a strong disposition in other parts of the Hall towards an angry but not unreasonable protest.
In case any portion of the company should be under the necessity of leaving before the close of the Reading in the apprehension of losing railway trains, they are respectfully entreated as an act of consideration and courtesy towards the remainder, to avail themselves of the opportunity afforded by the interval between the parts when Mr. Dickens retires for five minutes.
[P. T. O.

by his popular reception at the very time when the students of Glasgow University voted him into a humiliating third place in the election for their rector, on the grounds that he was 'a vulgar cockney, with the heart and manners of a Snob,' and a 'cowardly calumniator, the cuckoo of his own merits'.

From the standpoint of Dickens' emotions as well as his pocket the tour was an enormous success. Smith, his manager, bruised his legs black and blue with the weighty bag of sovereigns he carried round. When a hotel manager asked if Smith could give him some silver change from the takings, Smith handed over forty pounds without hesitation. No wonder Dickens was back on the road in a new tour of readings with fresh material in 1861. The takings continued to roll in, and Dickens continued to win richly earned plaudits.

He had taken a good deal of trouble in the preparation of his texts. He had selected with care passages from the novels which made up complete narrative incidents or satisfactorily self-contained monologues. Then, in red and blue inks, he had written stage directions for himself in the margins and scored the text with underlining and big balloons around phrases and words of special importance. All his acting talents were brilliantly employed as he alone, in evening dress, standing at a reading table, peopled the stage with different characters, different voices, different mannerisms. His fingers drummed on the desk as he described dancers at a ball; his face contracted into the mean, pinched sneer of Scrooge, and expanded again into the complacent beaming moon of a London alderman; his voice wheezed the ginny snuffle of Mrs Gamp or rose to a convincing childish falsetto for little Paul Dombey. Yet for all the astonishing acclaim his own characterisation won he was not above taking advice from sympathetic critics. Frith, the painter of *Derby Day*, was disappointed to find Sam Weller sounding tentative and uncertain in the trial scene from Pickwick. He mentioned this to Dickens, and by the next performance Sam's impertinent evidence was whipping out like pistol shots.

"Now, Mr Weller," said serjeant Buzfuz.
"Now, Sir" replied Sam.
"I believe you are in the service of Mr Pickwick the defendant in this case. Speak up, if you please, Mr Weller."
"I mean to speak up, Sir," replied Sam, "I am in the service o' that 'ere gen'l'man, and a wery good service it is."
"Little to do, and plenty to get, I suppose?" said serjeant Buzfuz, with jocularity.
"Oh, quite enough to get, Sir, as the soldier said ven they ordered him three hundred and fifty lashes," replied Sam.
"You must not tell us what the soldier, or any other man said, Sir," interposed the Judge, "it's not evidence."
"Wery good, my Lord," replied Sam.

At Newcastle he demonstrated his authority in a crisis. While the audience was listening attentively to the death of Smike the batten of gaslights above Dickens suddenly collapsed and fell on the platform with a crash. A woman screamed and ran out of her seat, and Dickens, looking at the crowded hall realised that a panic stampede of the three galleries full of people would cause much loss of life. So he laughed lightly and coolly asked the lady to return to her place, although his stage crew, terrified at the possibility of fire, trembled so much as they put things right that the platform shook under him. 'The more you want of the master,' said the lighting technician afterwards,' 'the more you'll find in him.'

But the triumph and the strain were taking their toll of Dickens' health. Neuralgia was starting to affect him after his readings, and gout attacked his left foot. With characteristic determination he persuaded his doctor that his foot was troubled by nothing worse than a bunion, disregarded warnings that his heart needed examination, and embarked on a new round of readings in 1866 with a more efficient manager, George Dolby. Big, bald, whiskery and jolly, Dolby was described by Mark Twain as 'a gladsome gorilla'.

Even his efficiency could not save Dickens from another close shave with the gas lighting. In Birmingham a heavy metal reflector was hung on copper wire over his head. A badly placed gas jet flared over the wire and made it red hot as the evening went on with the risk that the reflector might crash into the stalls, injuring members of the audience and perhaps starting a fire. Dolby peered anxiously round the screen behind Dickens whispering 'how long shall you be?' Dickens casually raised two fingers, but Dolby had no idea whether this meant two minutes, two sentences, two paragraphs, or two pages. In fact, Dickens stopped with no sign of hurry after two seconds. He had seen the danger in the middle of his reading, and had skilfully shortened and abridged the remainder of the passage in accordance with his own calculation of how long the wire would last.

With a competent manager, there was no reason why he should not make an attempt on the fat pickings of America. Dolby was sent over in 1867 to sound out the possibility of readings in Boston and New York. His report was favourable; a minority of the Anglophobe press tried to arouse hostile memories of the *American Notes* and *Martin Chuzzlewit*, but the younger generation was not interested in defending American society of twenty years earlier, and thousands of enthusiastic readers welcomed the notion of hearing Dickens in the flesh.

So in 1868 Dickens sailed to Boston for the second time in his life. He was annoyed on landing to find that waiters peered at him from the door while he dined;

Right:
The divine Sairey, one of the star characters in Dickens' readings, drinking with her friend Mrs Prig. From the drawing by Phiz for Martin Chuzzlewit.

Mrs Gamp propoges a toast.

Scrooge's third Visitor

he feared a repetition of the invasion of his privacy which had been so offensive in 1842. But Dolby's news was good. Queuing for tickets to hear Dickens had begun the night before the box office opened; an hour before opening time the queue was already half a mile long; all tickets were sold out in a hectic eleven hours and fourteen thousand dollars were taken in for the first reading in Boston. Dolby sold tickets at two dollars each. Scalpers were re-selling them at anything up to twenty-six dollars!

Longfellow was an old friend to be visited in Boston; like Dickens, he had aged and now looked 'like the very spirit of Christmas'. R. H. Dana and his father were friends who recalled the earlier American visit, and other distinguished Bostonians– the poet James Russell Lowell, Oliver Wendell Holmes and Ralph Waldo Emerson–renewed their earlier acquaintance. An interesting murder had been committed at Harvard, where Professor Webster had killed a colleague and then attempted to dispose of the body by dissecting it in his medical laboratory. A visit to so distinguished a scene of crime was heartily enjoyed by Dickens.

The readings in Boston, New York and Washington were a great success. True, one confident New Englander asserted that Dickens knew no more about Sam Weller 'n a cow does of pleatin' a shirt'. But a German janitor in New York produced a crescendo of praise: 'Mr Digguns, you are gread, mein herr. There is no ent to you. Bedder and bedder. Wot negst!'

In Washington President Andrew Johnson brought his entourage to hear the readings every day for a week. A small dog also got in one night in Washington and kept looking at Dickens intently from different parts of the house. In the end he broke down in a helpless fit of laughter and the audience joined him as the dog gave a bark from the centre aisle.

But the tour nearly killed Dickens. Strain ravaged his health and his throat had to be mustard-poulticed as his voice wore out. Dolby was amazed that his chief was always able to deliver his readings, in spite of colds and hoarseness in the daytime. By the end of the tour Dickens had a cough so permanent that he feared his lungs were injured, and, as he admitted in a letter to Mamie, was confined to an almost entirely liquid diet: 'At seven in the morning, in bed, a tumbler of cream and two tablespoons full of rum. At twelve, a sherry cobbler and a biscuit. At three (dinner time), a pint of champagne. At five minutes to eight, an egg beaten up with a glass of sherry. Between the parts, the strongest beef tea that can be made, drunk hot. At a quarter past ten, soup, and anything to drink that I can fancy. I don't eat more than half a pound of solid

food in the whole twenty four hours, if so much.'

The glittering success of the tour, which netted Dickens £20,000, and would have made double the amount if the dollar exchange rate had not been temporarily unfavourable after the American Civil War, persuaded him to dismiss medical warnings again and arrange a further series of lucrative readings for the autumn of 1868 in England.

During the summer, while Dickens was peacefully preparing new reading material at Gad's Hill, Charley, who was working in the library, heard what he took to be a tramp beating his wife outside. He paid no attention at first, but the racket increased, and at last Charley leapt up, convinced that he must interfere in what was evidently a brutal assault. He dashed out into the meadow and found—his father. 'Bill, dear Bill,' he was crying, in a woman's voice, 'you cannot have the heart to kill me. Oh! think of all I have given up, only this one night, for you. You *shall* have time to think, and save yourself this crime; I will not lose my hold, you cannot throw me off. Bill, Bill, for dear God's sake, for your own, for mine, stop before you spill my blood! I have been true to you, upon my guilty soul I have!' Dickens was creating the *pièce de resistance* of his public readings, the murder of Nancy by Bill Sykes.

'What do you think about it?' he asked Charley at dinner. 'The finest thing I have ever heard', was Charley's answer, 'but don't do it.' He could see that the intense excitement that this violent and melodramatic scene caused his father could not but injure his health, perhaps fatally. Dickens insisted on at least a private reading to try it out; a hundred friends heard the brilliant recreation of Fagin's spying on the virtuous prostitute Nancy, were terrified by the rising rage of Bill Sykes and his brutal murder of the girl, and felt their blood chill as they followed Sykes' guilty flight from the haunting memory of his victim till he reached his final squalid end on a rope in a riverside slum. Before the audience had got its breath back, Dickens' stage crew pulled aside screens and revealed a huge table of oysters and champagne. As the guests drank they congratulated the reader: 'The public have been looking for a sensation these last fifty years or so', a distinguished actress told him, 'and by Heaven they have got it!' 'I am bound to tell you that I had an almost irresistible impulse upon me to *scream*', was the tribute of a clergyman, 'and that, if anyone had cried out, I am certain I should have followed.'

'Well, Charley,' Dickens murmured to his son, 'and what do you think of it now?'

'It is finer even than I expected,' said the young man, 'but I still say, don't do it.'

Dickens seized Edmund Yates who was wandering past. 'What do you think of this, Edmund?' he asked. 'Here is Charley saying it is the finest thing he has ever heard, but persists in telling me, without giving any reason, not to do it.' Yates looked at father and son before saying gravely, 'I agree with Charley, Sir.'

But Dickens refused to believe that he was or could

DOLBY.—" *Well, Mr. Dickens, on the eve of our departure, I present you with $300,000, the result of your Lectures in America.*"
DICKENS.—" *What! only $300,000 ? Is that all I have made out of these penurious Yankees, after all my abuse of them ? Pshaw! Let us go, Dolby!*"

Some Americans never forgave Dickens for the criticism levelled at their country in American Notes *and* Martin Chuzzlewit.
Left:
Impressions of the last series of public readings.

Above:
Dickens reading.
Right:
Dickens' Dream, *a painting which attempts to show*
Dickens with the products of his imagination.

Left:
Dickens exhausted by the Sikes and Nancy reading, from a sketch by H. Furniss.
Right:
Sketches giving an impression of how Dickens aged under the strain of public reading. He was only fifty-eight when he died.

be seriously weakened. He desperately wanted audiences in the palm of his hand, and he knew he could get them with this great, sensational, frightening reading. He insisted on touring with the 'Murder', although its invariable effect was to exhaust him to the point of frustration. After each reading he limped away to his dressing room, where he collapsed on to a sofa unable to speak for some time. His doctors discovered that his pulse reached alarming rates when he read the 'Murder'. Dolby pleaded with him to do a number of readings without including the 'Murder'. Dickens' reaction was alarming. He leapt from his seat at the dinner table, hurled his knife and fork down so violently that they smashed his plate to pieces, and shouted, 'Dolby, your infernal caution will be your ruin one of these days.' Never before had he spoken rudely, or even angrily, to any member of his entourage in Dolby's hearing. In two minutes he was weeping and apologising to his manager, though he was never willing to take the sensible advice and abandon the 'Murder' readings altogether.

A critical professional eye confirmed his belief that the 'Murder' reading was an artistic triumph. Old Macready, now aged seventy-five, came to hear the reading in Cheltenham. Afterwards in the dressing room he was almost overcome and made a tremulous comparison of the 'Murder' reading with his own greatest role: 'In my–er–best times–er–you remember them, my dear boy–er–gone, gone!–no, it comes to this–er–TWO MACBETHS!' It was a touching reward for Dickens' consideration in taking his tour off-course to make it accessible to his friend in his retirement. But mental triumph could not disguise the approach of physical collapse. His lame foot was being treated with fomentations of poppy-heads and a special boot; he found difficulty in keeping his balance and suffered from attacks of giddiness; his left hand hardly seemed under his control and was hard for him to raise; and when these symptoms were reported to Francis Beard, his family physician, he raced from London to Liverpool and insisted that Dickens must read no more. A distinguished consultant, Sir Thomas Watson, confirmed Beard's diagnosis that Dickens was on the brink of paralysis of his entire left side together with a possible apoplexy. The tour was cut short, and Dickens gave no more than a handful of farewell readings later the following year. It is, perhaps, astonishing evidence of the psychological hold living audiences had over him that even the doctors who recognised for a fact that public reading was killing Dickens felt compelled, nonetheless, to allow him the hope of his last few farewell appearances.

The End

Tavistock House was sold after Katey's marriage. Dickens made do with rented accommodation for the winter season in London, and passed the last years of his life at Gad's Hill. His books were brought down to Rochester and installed, together with the shelves full of dummy books for which he had invented facetious titles. Many of his opinions and prejudices were reflected in these painted wooden bindings: *Hansard's Guide to Refreshing Sleep* indicated his contempt for parliament; twenty-one volumes of the *History of a Short Chancery Suit* echoed *Bleak House's* objection to the laws delays; *Socrates on Wedlock* was hard on Kate, who could not really be described as a Xanthippe; and his hatred of that conservatism which looked back to supposedly good old days was evinced in *King Henry the Eighth's Evidences of Christianity* and the series *The Wisdom of Our Ancestors*: I *Ignorance*, II *Superstition*, III *The Block*, IV *The Stake*, V *The Rack*, VI *Dirt*, VII *Disease*. A Victorian liberal's buoyant moral optimism was displayed in the preposterously narrow volume *The Virtues of Our Ancestors* which was placed alongside their '*Wisdom*'.

His pride in his house and its literary connection was shown in a plaque he placed on the landing; 'This House, GAD'S HILL PLACE, stands on the summit of Shakespeare's Gad's Hill, ever memorable for its association with Sir John Falstaff in his noble

Above:
Millais' drawing of Dickens in death.
Left:
Dickens' desk, now in Dickens House, with various personal belongings on it. The inkstand, china monkey and glass were Dickens own; the card case was a present from him to his wife; miniature of Katey Dickens; nineteenth-century handkerchief from Dickens House.

fancy. *But, my lads, my lads, tomorrow morning, by four o'clock, early at Gad's Hill! there are pilgrims going to Canterbury with rich offerings and traders riding to London with fat purses; I have vizards for you all; you have horses for yourselves.'*

In summer the house was filled with visitors whose well-furnished rooms always included books, writing paper and frequent changes of quill pens, kettles and tea-cups, and the cane-bottomed chairs which Dickens preferred to plush upholstery. The walls of the house were hung with mirrors, Hogarth prints, and paintings by Stansfield. The garden was rich with honeysuckle, nasturtiums, brilliant red geraniums, and mignonette.

Here it was that Ellen Ternan came to visit him, and, to Katey's jealous indignation, was allowed the unique privilege of going into his study in the mornings while he was working. By the eighteen-sixties Ellen had become his mistress, a fact which was kept with some difficulty from her mother and sisters. Dickens provided her with a house of her own in Peckham where he visited her, and in the summer of 1865 she shared an alarming adventure with him.

They were returning from Paris where he had been able to snatch a week's holiday after completing the publication arrangements for his last completed novel, *Our Mutual Friend*. The Channel crossing was calm and the air balmy when Dickens and Ellen reached Folkestone in the early afternoon. They boarded a train to London and were spinning merrily through Kent at fifty miles an hour when, between Headcorn and Staplehurst, the train approached a group of workmen on the line. Through a horrible error in timetabling gangers were replacing worn timbers at a little bridge on the wrong day, and in a moment half the train had leapt off a gap in the rails and plunged

violently down the river bank. Without warning
Dickens and Ellen found their carriage 'off the rail
and beating the ground as the car of a half-emptied
balloon might do'. Ellen screamed, and an old lady
who was in the compartment with them cried out,
'My God!' Dickens firmly caught hold of both ladies
and said, 'We can't help ourselves, but we can be
quiet and composed. Pray don't cry out.' The old lady
was calmed at once, and in a moment their carriage
came to rest at an awkward angle. Dickens told his
companions not to move so as not to overbalance the
carriage. Then he himself clambered out of the
window and ordered two guards who were running
pointlessly up and down to fetch keys and open the
carriage doors. When he had seen Ellen and the old
lady to safety he filled his hat with water which he
took to the injured and dying. He behaved like a hero
in this accident, but a minimum of publicity was given
to the event, both then and later, by those intimates
who knew who his companion had been.

On his trip to America two years later Dickens
hoped to smuggle Ellen out as a companion. He had to
find out first of all whether he could cope with her
presence on top of his round of public readings and

*Dickens helping the injured at the Staplehurst railway
disaster.*

engagements; then an elaborate coded cable to Wills
was to be forwarded to Ellen who would know
whether to cross the Atlantic and join Dickens or not.
In the event, the telegram Wills did receive read, 'Safe
and well. Expect good letter full of hope.' 'Safe and
well' was the direction to Ellen to stay where she was;
she was only to join her lover if the telegram included
the words 'all well'.

The consummation of his love for Ellen must have
brought Dickens unhappiness as well as satisfaction.
His temperament was domestic and respectable; he
could never have followed his young friend Wilkie
Collins in openly keeping a mistress, however much he
shared Collins' distaste for the 'unco' guid'. A lively
little girl who introduced herself to him on a train in
America and who revealed a heartwarming familiarity
with his works may have touched Dickens on a tender
spot. She asked him whether he cried when reading
aloud: "We all do in our family," she told him, 'and
we never read about Tiny Tim, or about Steerforth
when his body is washed up on the beach, on Satur-

day nights, or our eyes are too swollen to go to Sunday School.' 'Yes,' returned Dickens in a low voice, 'I cry when I read about Steerforth.' Not Tiny Tim, the tear-jerking cripple; not one of his great sentimental successes, Little Nell or Paul Dombey; but Steerforth, the brilliant, promising, handsome seducer of a poor bedazzled maiden moved Dickens to the tears he could admit to a strange child.

The more innocent friendship with Mary Boyle was kept up, too, throughout this period. She continued to send him his colourful daily buttonholes–an elaborate one comprising a camellia surrounded with violets excited comment at a farewell dinner given for Dickens before his departure for America. The travelling reader had been surprised to find his buttonholes awaiting him as usual at hotels in Scotland and Dublin; he was even more delighted when Mary managed to have them delivered to him wherever he went in America. This was quite a feat on her part when the telegraphic ordering of flowers was not a normal commercial service, and the Boston newspapers scented a middle-aged romance when they heard about it. 'Oh, Charles,' they twitted him, 'at your age and with that bald head and that grey goatee!' Georgina wisely remained

Gad's Hill Place.

friendly with these two women, though her undoubted knowledge that Charles' friendship with Ellen was not entirely innocent led Katey to say later, 'Auntie Georgie was not quite straight.'

A melancholy series of deaths robbed Dickens of many of his friends during the eighteen-sixties. The older generation of writers who had welcomed a young man to their midst–Jeffrey, Leigh Hunt, Rogers–had long passed away. Leech and Maclise died; Stansfield compelled a reconciliation between Lemon and Dickens on his death bed; before long Lemon followed him to the grave. Macready was out of reach in retirement in Dorset. And Forster's growing pomposity and self-importance was gradually alienating him more and more from Dickens. When Macready's favourite daughter died Dickens was appalled by the self-centred grief Forster displayed. 'You may imagine the shock and blow it was to ME', Forster had said. 'Me! me! me!' Dickens expostulated. 'As if there were no poor, old, broken friend in the case!' What was worse, Forster had once called Miss Macready 'a very offensive and improper young per-

son', so that Dickens could now uncharitably view his grief as humbug.

With new friends there could never be quite the same intimacy that had existed in the circle of the eighteen-forties. Dickens was now too established a figure to find new intimates with whom he could rest at ease or in a position of equality. He was likely to be the patron for younger men : whereas he had observed from the outside Egg's attempt to woo Georgina (the little painter was another who died in this decade), he actively encouraged Percy Fitzgerald in his ambition to marry Mamie. Mamie refused, and Dickens and Forster enjoyed a jocular and avuncular flirtation with the pretty young lady Fitzgerald did ultimately marry.

An attachment which displeased Dickens' young English admirers began one night in Paris when he went to see *La Dame Aux Camellias* at the theatre. Charles Fechter's performance as Armand brought the house down, and Dickens urged the young man to come to London. In 1863 the French actor triumphantly showed London new ways of approaching Shakespeare. He cut away a lot of traditional ham from *Hamlet*, and created an Iago stripped of his normal Demon King-like hissing and sneering which, of course, made considerably more sense of *Othello*. From 1868 to 1865 he was one of the most frequent visitors to Gad's Hill Place and Dickens willingly advised him on literary matters and the alteration of scripts. And when one of those financial crises so common in lavish theatrical productions overtook Fechter, Dickens tactfully put three thousand pounds in the hands of his manager and Fechter was saved from experiencing bankruptcy as the reward of art. He found a charming way of expressing his gratitude, though he puzzled the Gad's Hill servants sorely.

'The fifty-eight boxes have come, sir', Dickens' groom informed him as his master arrived at Higham railway station one afternoon.

'What ?' asked Dickens.

'The fifty-eight boxes have come, sir', repeated the man.

Dickens looked in bewilderment at his servant. 'I know nothing of fifty-eight boxes.'

'Well, sir,' said the groom ominously, 'they are all piled up outside the gate and we shall soon see, sir.'

Fifty-eight large and mysterious packing cases there were indeed at Gad's Hill; when they were opened they revealed ninety-four variously shaped pieces of timber. These could be slotted together like an elaborate constructional toy to form a little two-storey

Left :
This advertisement, making use of Dickens' image to promote pens, also has the signatures of many of his friends embodied in it.

Right :
The Wooden Midshipman. The London ship's-instrument-maker's sign Dickens incorporated into Dombey and Son. *Now exhibited at Dickens House, Doughty Street.*

Swiss chalet. It was a present from Fechter, and when the chalet was erected he completed his gift by paying for its furniture. Dickens was delighted, and used the upper room as a summer study from which he could look out on his trees and land at Gad's Hill.

The theatre was still part of Dickens' life, although he was now too lame to act himself or be more than stage manager for even the most domestic of private theatricals. But his acquaintance among theatre people remained large : once again, he was now more nearly a grand old man of the theatre than the professionals he mixed with. Pirated and authorised versions of his writings had appeared continuously on the Victorian stage, and there was hardly an actor who had not at some time or other in his career done something from Dickens. Indeed there were some who had built successful careers very largely around the presentation of Dickens' characters. J. L. Toole, for example, repeatedly played the Artful Dodger, Serjeant Buzfuz, Captain Cuttle, Bob Cratchit, and Caleb Plummer (Caleb Plummer, the sentimental old toy maker with a blind daughter from *The Cricket on the Hearth*, is a Dickens character rarely preferred by twentieth-century readers ; but he was a great favourite with nineteenth-century actors for whom the Christmas books offered rewarding material.) It was in connection with *A Christmas Carol* that Toole told Dickens a stage story which moved the writer considerably. Toole had been playing Bob Cratchit, and had, in the Christmas dinner scene, to carve up a goose and a

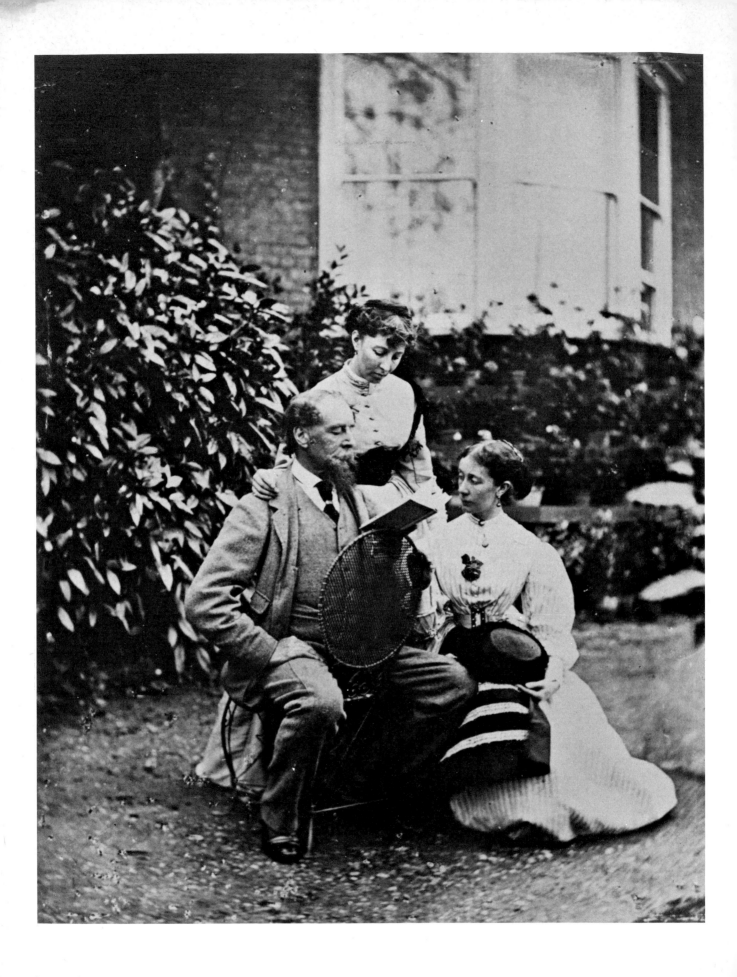

plum pudding to distribute among his numerous
'family'. The management supplied a real goose and a
real pudding each night, and Toole was amazed by the
avidity with which the stage children (mostly the offspring of scene-shifters) gobbled up the food he put
on their plates. Most surprising of all was the delicate
and attractive little girl playing Tiny Tim. It seemed
impossible to give Tiny Tim too much food. Whatever
was heaped onto the little cripple's plate was taken
over to the painted fireside and apparently despatched.
Toole found himself conducting ridiculous experiments on stage each night, heaping more and more
food onto the child's plate until, when the little girl
had apparently polished off an entire half-goose in
four or five minutes, he arranged to have her watched
and questioned. Then it became apparent that whatever Tiny Tim took back to his place was never eaten;
the little actress was pushing her food through the fire-
place behind the scenery to her sister who took it
away and shared it with the remainder of their im-
poverished family. 'Ah,' said Dickens sadly when he
was told, 'you should have given her the whole goose.'

When not patronising, Dickens could accept the
highest patronage. He breakfasted with Gladstone
while the latter was Prime Minister, and was introduced to Disraeli. Dickens and Disraeli had moved in
the same circle thirty years earlier (Lady Blessington,
for example, was a friend of both) but although they
had subsequently attended literary dinners together
they had never previously met with any degree
of intimacy. Dickens had always despised Disraeli's
romantic patriotic politics and was now amazed
to find that he liked the man very much indeed.
'A loss to literature' was his verdict on the novelist-
statesman.

The highest patronage came from Queen Victoria.
She met him at last in 1870, though with her usual in-
sensitivity she felt she had made a sufficient gesture
towards waiving protocol by remaining on her feet,
leaning across a sofa throughout the interview. This
meant that she kept an ageing man with severe gout on
his feet for ninety minutes. Nor was her presentation of
an autographed copy of her *Journal of Our Life in the
Highlands* a generous exchange for the complete set of
Dickens' works she demanded of him. A week later
Dickens went to the levée and shortly after that
Mamie was presented to the Queen. Georgina's
equivocal position in Dickens' household meant that
she could not be invited to court.

The Queen accepted a copy of the first number of
Dickens' new novel *Edwin Drood*. His love for the
quiet cathedral town of Rochester where his life was
drawing to a close found beautiful expression in it.
But though he might be tired he was not exhausted;
his work was not sinking into nostalgia or any repetition of past effects. Rather, he was proposing to outdo
the younger generation and write a mystery better than

The chalet Fechter gave Dickens.

those of Wilkie Collins. His old interests, murder and hypnotic powers, were adding excitement to his plot; and the use of a squalid waterside opium den as a setting allowed him to include fantastic oriental hallucinations in passages of superb bravura writing.

On 8 June he worked all day on *Drood* in the little chalet. At dinner, Georgina was alarmed by the pain and tiredness in his face. Suddenly he said he had to go at once to London, pushed back his crimson damask chair, and collapsed. Servants moved him to the dining room sofa, and doctors were summoned. The case was hopeless: a paralytic stroke from which there could be no recovery. Charley arrived in the house the next day, and Georgina also sent for Ellen Ternan and Mary Boyle. The family waited through the warm syringa-scented day, until at ten past six Dickens heaved a deep sigh and died.

His will contained his last demonstration against the empty pomp and circumstance with which his countrymen of his own class were surrounding their lives. He demanded a private unostentacious funeral, ordered 'that those who attend my funeral wear no scarf, cloak, black bow, long hat band, or other such revolting absurdity', and insisted that his tombstone must bear the plain inscription of his name without even an added Mr or Esquire. How recently it was, that he had entertained readers of *Edwin Drood* with his vigorous burlesque of Victorian monumental masonry:

ETHELINDA
Reverential Wife of
Mr. THOMAS SAPSEA,
AUCTIONEER, VALUER, ESTATE AGENT, &c.
OF THIS CITY,
Whose Knowledge of the World,
Though somewhat extensive,
Never brought him acquainted with
A SPIRIT
More capable of
LOOKING UP TO HIM.
STRANGER, PAUSE
And ask thyself the question,
CANST THOU DO LIKEWISE?
If Not,
WITH A BLUSH RETIRE

The nation demanded that its favourite writer should be buried in Westminster Abbey, and the Abbey authorities agreed to the quiet, private funeral he had demanded. John Forster, too deeply distressed to speak, was the last to leave the grave in poet's corner; he knew his friend would have preferred the quiet resting place he had expected outside Rochester cathedral.

A hansom cabman at the funeral expressed the national love and trust Dickens had earned: 'Ah, Mr Dickens was a great man', he said, 'and a true friend of the poor. We cabmen were always hoping he would do a turn for us one day.'

Right:
A British Railways poster for Yarmouth testifies to the perennial attraction of the Copperfield story.

THE LATE MR. CHARLES DICKENS.

The mere announcement that Charles Dickens is dead repeats the common sentence passed on all humanity. Death has once again demanded its own, and made a claim which all men must sooner or later meet. We forget how many mortals breathe their last in every minute according to the calculations of statistical authorities. Sufficient unto the day is the evil thereof, and yesterday, the 9th day of June, 1870, will be an evil day in the memories of all who can appreciate true genius and admire its matchless works. We have had greater writers both in poetry and prose, but they were not of our day and generation. For us just now this loss is our greatest. It would have been great at any time from the moment when he turned with aversion from the drudgery of a solicitor's office, amid the forebodings of his friends, and thenceforward rose in the clear light of literature, until he soared in the sunshine of success far above all his fellows. There are minds of such jealous fibre that the very merits of an author, his mightiest gifts and his most special talents, only serve as food on which to nourish their prejudices. Such are they who, while forced to admit the wit, humour, and power of Charles Dickens, always added, " but he was vulgar." Yes, in one sense he was vulgar ; he delighted in sketching the characters not of dukes and duchesses, but of the poor and lowly. He had listened to their wants and sorrows, seen them in their alleys and garrets, had learnt their accents and dialect by heart, and then, with a truth and liveliness all his own, he photographed them in his immortal works. In that sense alone was Charles Dickens " vulgar." He was of the people, and lived among them. His was not the close atmosphere of a saloon or of a forcing house. In the open air of the streets, and woods, and fields, he lived, and had his being, and so he came into closer union with common men, and caught with an intuitive force and fulness of feature every detail of their daily life. His creations have become naturalized, so to speak, among all classes of the community, and are familiar to every man, high or low. How many fine gentlemen and ladies, who never saw Pickwick or Sam Weller in the flesh, have laughed at their portraits by Charles Dickens. How many have been heartbroken at the sufferings of Oliver, been indignant at the brutality of Bill Sykes, wept over the fallen Nancy's cruel fate, and even sympathized with the terrible agony of Fagin in the condemned cell, who but for Charles Dickens would never have known that such sorrows and crimes, such

expression of his face,
for medical assistance.
it with imperfect arti
ment he complained of
to the side of his
the window might be a
diately, and Miss Hog
took his arm, intending
After one or two steps
his left side, and remain
less until his death, w
past 6 on Thursday, ju
As soon as he fell a tele
old friend and constant
Carr Beard, of Welbeck
Hill immediately, but f
patient to be past hope.
already in attendance ;
wentdownonThursday, M
until the last. The pupil
dilated, that of the left
stertorous, the limbs fe
before death, when s
These symptoms point
way of a blood-vessel in
quent large hemorrhage,
what is called apoplexy.
post-mortem examination

FOREIGN ARTISTS
ACAD

TO THE EDITOR
Sir,—I regret to be ob
tively the official statemen
Royal Academy which app
8th inst.
I assert and, if necessa
picture was delivered at th
Messrs. Bource and Mo
this city, and whose work
Will the Royal Academ
picture was placed on the
was taken away from the
marked in chalk on the b
Is this not sufficient pr
after full deliberation ?
I am, Sir, your o
J. VAN LERIO
à l'Acad
54, Rue Vieille Bourse, Anv

THE CASE OF D

TO THE EDITOR
Sir.—It was only this afte
published in *The Times* on
much, as I should have be
immediate reply. That
than a reproduction of

Obituary 1970

9 June, 1970

The death occurred, one hundred years ago today, at his home near Rochester, of Mr Charles Dickens the writer. His rise to fame was rapid, but he never forgot his humble origins and never lost touch with the essential tastes and sympathies of ordinary people. For nearly forty years his position as England's leading novelist was hardly challenged.

He left an extensive family and body of friends who for many years did all that lay in their power to keep his memory green and protect his reputation. His friend and adviser, John Forster, published a three-volume *Life* which told readers for the first time of the novelist's experience of manual labour in a blacking factory at the age of twelve. But Forster and the Dickens family agreed to say as little as possible about the unhappy breakdown of Mr Dickens' marriage, and for fifty years very few people knew anything of the great writer's liaison in his last years with Miss Ellen Ternan, an actress.

At the time of Mr Dickens' death a new generation of young critics was beginning to question the value of his work. His attack on the civil service in *Little Dorrit* had offended the intellectually powerful Stephen family, and well into the twentieth century circles in Bloomsbury and Cambridge continued to dismiss his writings as vulgar and inartistic.

Defenders have never been wanting however. Writers of social realism from George Gissing and Bernard Shaw in the eighteen-nineties to George Orwell in the nineteen-forties have recognised Dickens as an ancestor. For the first fifty years after his death, though, Dickens' admirers were more of the type of G. K. Chesterton. They saw their idol as the prophet of a jolly, good-humoured, generous way of life, and made no bones about the fact that they thought his talent had ebbed towards the end of his life as his books became less funny. These admirers tended to devote a great deal of time to finding quaint Victorian byways which they took to be the originals of locales in the novels. Thus the 'Old Curiosity Shop' was identified in Portsmouth Street, despite Dickens' own assertion that the building no longer existed when he wrote. The Dickens Fellowship was founded in honour of the 'Immortal Memory', and such extra-ordinary junketings as a mock trial, undertaken by literary men and presided over by G. K. Chesterton, which it was hoped might solve the mystery of *Edwin Drood*, were staged. The first thirty years of the twentieth century were a notable period for fancy dress coach tours and dinners, recreating the nostalgic view of pre-industrial England which could be extracted from a very selective reading of Dickens.

Critical attitudes towards Dickens began to change in the nineteen-thirties and were stimulated by the revelations then made about Ellen Ternan. American critics were quick to notice that Charles Dickens was suffering from a lack of serious attention in his own country, and they pointed out that the previously despised late novels contained a mature and challenging picture of life powerful enough almost to outweigh the vitality of the early comedy.

The wider public, meanwhile, had never lost sight of Dickens' qualities as an entertainer. Plays and films kept his plots and characters well known, even to people who had never read a word he had written. Radio found that serialised readings or dramatisations from the novels entertained the listener, and B.B.C. television has presented serial dramatisations of more novels by Dickens than any other classic English writer.

To the Memory of
CHARLES DICKENS,
(ENGLAND'S MOST POPULAR AUTHOR,)
Who died at his residence, Higham, near Rochester, Kent,
JUNE 9TH, 1870,
Aged 58 Years.
HE WAS A SYMPATHISER WITH THE POOR, THE SUFFERING, AND
THE OPPRESSED; AND
BY HIS DEATH, ONE OF ENGLAND'S GREATEST WRITERS IS LOST
TO THE WORLD.

Printed at J. H. WOODLEY'S FUNERAL TABLET OFFICE, 30, Fore Street, City,
London.

A memorial card for Dickens, issued after his death.

Right:
*Mr. Pickwick was given a warm welcome by the popular
journals on his first appearance and continued for many
years to lend his name to a strange variety of consumer
goods. A poster for jam, probably early in this century.*

This popular appeal affects our lives even if we choose to avoid its appearance on stage and screen. The strong impact of Dickens' combination of colourful characters in a bygone age has left its mark on popular art. Dickensian souvenirs and curios are constantly being mass produced: Toby jugs of Dickens characters, and all the artefacts of the gift trade from bookmarks to dishcloths. Advertising frequently exploits the original imagination of Charles Dickens, confidently expecting that his characters will be recognised by a wide audience and will evoke appropriate emotional associations. Interior decorators, particularly in pubs and restaurants, love to suggest the 'coaching-days' settings of Dickens' novels. The writer who could always describe the poor man's feast of oysters and stout with gusto while the rich man's caviare and champagne left him unmoved, is an obviously suitable patron for popular eating places. The copper coach horns, horse brasses and polished wood and leather we associate with so many drinking places today reflect a national recognition of Dickens as a writer for whom drink was a social pleasure, not a drug, and a pleasure to which everyone was entitled.

But it is at Christmas that we pay our most powerful tribute to the memory of Charles Dickens. The Victorian Christmas was almost his single-handed in-

vention: even the commercial practice of catering to an artificially extended market at Yuletide was initiated by Dickens in the creation of special Christmas Books. Christmas celebrations which focus on family life and children owe much to this writer who repeatedly placed his most powerful moral comments in the mouths of children or close-knit families. If you want to know how and when your Christmas dinner menu took its present shape, look at *A Christmas Carol* and see what Scrooge gave Bob Cratchit! And then compare that with Mr Pickwick's food at Dingley Dell.

After one hundred years Dickens' reputation is no longer in doubt. He towers over nineteenth-century English literature without a rival. Critics and readers of many different kinds today pay him the highest compliment that can be given an English writer: he is the only novelist to whom we frequently apply the adjective Shakespearian.

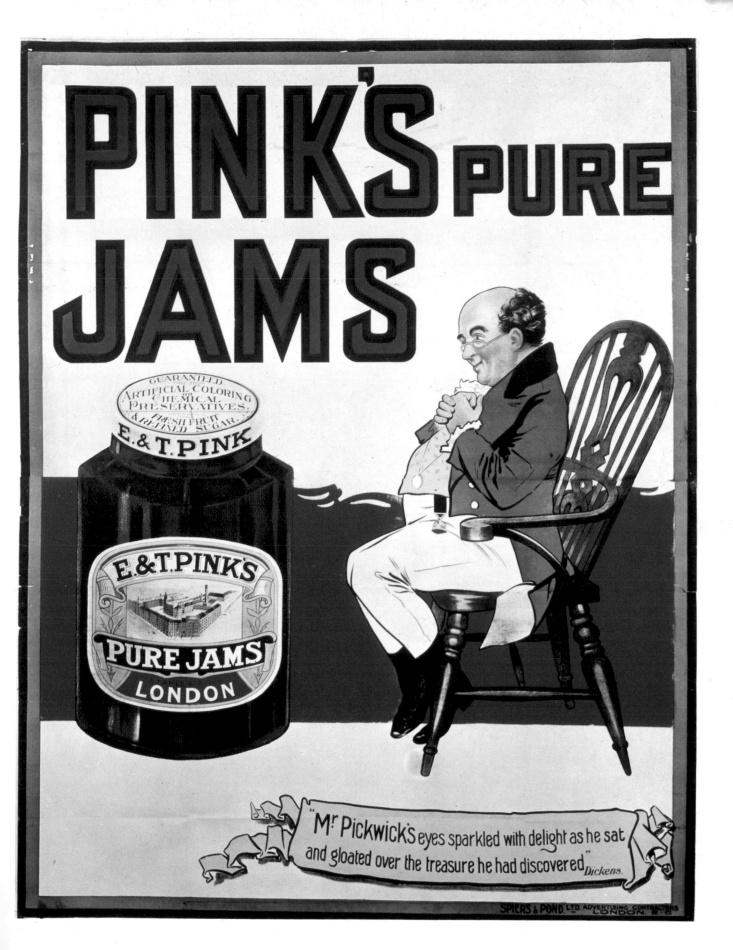

I. W. Burford.

132

Left :
Beerbohm Tree as Fagin.
Right :
Henry Irving as Mr Jingle in Pickwick.
Below :
Mr. Pickwick is shown his cell in prison, where he has landed after a breach of promise action brought by his landlady.
Still from the Renown production of Pickwick Papers, *starring James Hayter, reproduced by courtesy of Renown Pictures.*

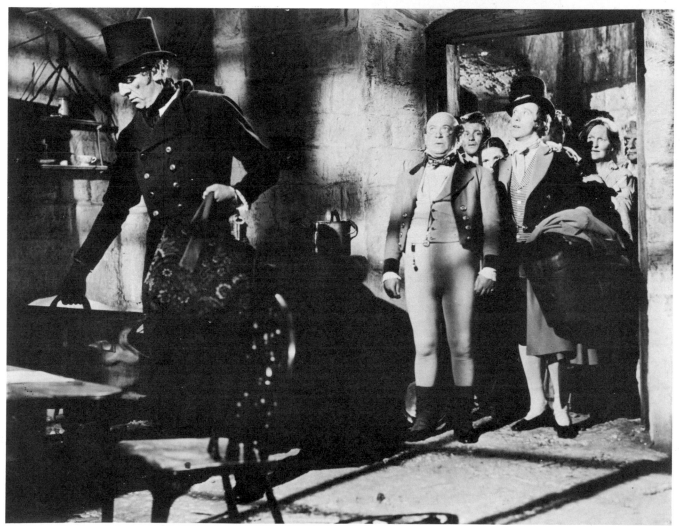

Some Major Dates and Events

1812 Born at Landport.
1817 Family moved to Chatham.
1822 Family moved to London.
1824 Warren's Blacking Factory episode.
1827 Clerk at Ellis and Blackmore, attorneys.
1828 Freelance reporter in Doctors' Commons.
In love with Maria Beadnell.
1832 Parliamentary reporter.
1833 *A Dinner at Poplar Walk* published.
1836 Married Catherine Hogarth.
Sketches by Boz.
Pickwick Papers, 1836-37.
1837 Charles Dickens jr. born.
48 Doughty St acquired.
Mary Hogarth died.
Oliver Twist, 1837-38.
1838 Mary Dickens born.
Grimaldi's memoirs edited.
Nicholas Nickleby, 1838-39.
1839 Kate Macready Dickens born.
1 Devonshire Terrace leased.
1840 *Master Humphrey's Clock.*
The Old Curiosity Shop.
1841 Walter Landor Dickens born.
Barnaby Rudge.
1842 First Visit to America.
American Notes.
1843 *Martin Chuzzlewit*, 1843-44.
A Christmas Carol.
1844 Francis Jeffrey Dickens born.
Met Christiana Weller.
Family moved to Italy.
The Chimes.
1845 Alfred D'Orsay Tennyson Dickens born.
The Cricket on the Hearth.

1846 *Daily News* established.
Dombey and Son,
Family in Switzerland, 1846-48.
The Battle of Life.
1847 Sydney Smith Haldimand Dickens born.
1849 Henry Fielding Dickens born.
David Copperfield, 1849-50.
1850 Dora Annie Dickens born.
Household Words established.
1851 Dora Annie died.
Tavistock House acquired.
1852 Edward Bulwyer Lytton Dickens born.
Bleak House, 1852-53.
1854 *Hard Times.*
1855 Met Maria (Beadnell) Winter.
Little Dorrit, 1855-57.
1856 Gadshill purchased.
1858 First public readings.
Garrick Club row.
Separation from Catherine Dickens.
1859 *All the Year Round* established.
A Tale of Two Cities.
1860 *Great Expectations*, 1860-61.
1862 Second series of readings.
1863 Walter Dickens died in India.
1864 *Our Mutual Friend*, 1864-65.
1866 Third series of readings.
1867 Second visit to America.
1868 Last series of readings.
1870 *Edwin Drood* started.
Died at Gadshill.

Acknowledgements

We wish to thank particularly the Dickens Fellowship and the Trustees of Dickens House who generously put at our disposal their picture collection and museum exhibits.

Key to picture positions: (T) top, (B) bottom, (L) left, (R) right. Numbers refer to the pages on which the pictures appear.

British Rail 127; Brown Brothers 55 (BL & BR), 57 (T & B), 111; Colindale Newspaper Library 23, 128; Corporation of the City of Rochester 64, 96, 107, 114, 130; Culver Pictures 56; Alec Davis Designers 15 (B); Dickens Fellowship and Trustees of Dickens House 15 (T), 19 (B), 33 (TR), 34, 37 (T & B), 39, 48, 49, 50 (B), 51, 52 (T), 53 (B), 54, 60, 65 (T), 66 (T), 80 (B), 86, 87 (T), 88, 92, 95, 97, 98, 99, 100, 101, 104, 112, 113, 114-115, 117 (T & B), 118, 119, 120, 122, 123, 124, 126, 131; Peter Fairfoul 68, 91; Forster Collection 40, 58, 78, 79, endpapers; by kind permission of the London Museum 36 (T & B), 89; Mansell Collection 17 (BR), 18, 19 (T), 21, 32, 35, 41, 42, 43, 44, 45, 47, 50 (T), 52 (B), 63, 66 (B), 70, 72, 80 (T), 82 (T), 83 (T), 87 (B), 105, 106, 109, 110, 121; Mary Evans Picture Library 14; National Portrait Gallery 33 (B), 53 (T), 83 (B), 116; Radio Times Hulton Picture Library 11, 16 (T), 27, 29 (T), 55 (T), 59, 65 (B), 75, 76 (T), 77, 82 (B), 102, 125; Raymond Mander and Joe Mitcheson Theatre Collection 17 (BL), 30, 31 (T & B), 38, 132, 133 (T); Renown Pictures 133 (B); Tate Gallery 10 (B), 29 (B), 69; Trustees of the British Museum 10 (TL & TR), 12, 13, 16 (B), 17 (T), 20, 24, 25, 26, 28, 46, 61, 67, 71, 73, 76 (B); Victoria and Albert Museum 22, 84 (T), 85, 93.

Index

"But here's a lark—" considering—
"Deputy tomorrow morning? Blest if the air
the window his coat, and smiles his legs in

"How do you know that, Deputy?"

"Cos Castle told me so just a
minute o' purpose. She ses, 'Deputy, I must
I'm a goin to take a turn at the Kin-
with his former zest. and
eating alone on the pavement, breaks into a—
of the Dean

Mr Datchery receives the commu—
pondering face, and breaks up the conference
and sitting here over the supper
Mrs Tope has left prepared for him, he sti—
at length he rises, the door
chalked strokes on its inner side

"I like," says he, but
delighted with what is against him. He say
He sighs over the contemplation o—
the cupboard shelves, and pauses with it un—
addition to make to the account. "I think a un
satisfied in scoring up; "so, suits the ad—
goes to bed.

a brilliant morning.